A FOOD LOVER'S TREASURY

A FOOD LOVER'S TREASURY

JULIE RUGG & LYNDA MURPHY

FRANCES LINCOLN LIMITED
PUBLISHERS

A FOOD LOVER'S TREASURY

Frances Lincoln Limited
4 Torriano Mews
Torriano Avenue
London NW5 2RZ
www.franceslincoln.com

Introduction copyright © 2008 Lynda Murphy & Julie Rugg
For full acknowledgments, see page 228

First Frances Lincoln edition: 2008

ISBN 13: 978-0-7112-2912-9

Printed and bound in China

2 4 6 8 9 7 5 3 1

CONTENTS

FOREWORD

This is a book about food, and the food that's in books. Tucked away in many great literary works are some essential truths on the subject of consumption: that someone is always disappointed when a tart is halved; that people dither when faced with too great a choice when it comes to cheese; that roasted udder is best kept a once-in-a-lifetime experience; that oranges should always be eaten in private; that toast is criminally under-appreciated, though even James Bond can't get enough of it; that, attended to properly, breakfast is by far the best meal of the day; and that it's a brave man who carves poultry in front of an audience. Other less well-known truths include the fact that kippers can be cooked on an iron; gravy expectation is high amongst commercial gentlemen; and every child at some time sees their name written in treacle.

This book is a running buffet of extracts and quotations on the subject of food broadly and diversely defined. It reflects a species of literary gluttony on our part. We both consume words with undue haste but it's nice to stop and savour – with the author – a taste or a meal or a clever observation about the ways we all eat. The ordering of the material here is nothing less than arbitrary, though occasionally it appears that spats break out on such subjects as the relative merits of tea over coffee, the virtue of music with meals, and whether the French can with clear conscience castigate English cooking. We hope our own preferences are not entirely obvious, so that the reader is free to make their own judgements on whether particular foods elicit a grin or a grimace.

Over the centuries, trends and themes recur with comforting regularity. Every age has its regrettable eating experiences, and places thought best to avoid. Smollett is scathing on the subject of food additives, and provides a less-than-savoury reminder that things weren't much better a couple of centuries ago than they are now. There is universal agreement that the simple and natural foods are the best. Foodie pretension is not a new phenomenon: even the most pompous contemporary gourmand has a long way to go before they can outclass the entirely black menu served by Huysman's decadent protagonist.

There is an index, in case anyone has a sudden urge to discover what the literary world has to say on the subject of pineapples (unappetizing with mashed potato, if you are wondering). The range of entries in the index is a sad indication of how confined our nutritional world has become. Things are changing. There is, currently, a rather self-congratulatory obsession with a return to traditional, rustic fare of the wriggling, smelly and visceral sort. But easily outdoing such machismo, Parson Woodforde, eighteenth-century diarist, remains the pre-eminent champion of extreme eaters. He was unstinting in his exploration of the nether regions of culinary experience, and we salute his bravery.

Above all these extracts demonstrate that food is one of the great overlooked themes of literature, and pursuing this theme is a good excuse to re-read some classics. Each of the quotations is fully referenced, so that the reader can 'source' the favoured titbits, and seek out further treats for themselves.

Julie Rugg

INTRODUCTION

The Food Lover's Treasury is a testament to our own idio-
syncratic love affairs with different kinds of food. Julie and
I both grew up in the 1970s – a decade in which, you have
to admit, Britain's diet was pretty awful. The legacy of postwar rationing seems to have been a fear of anything natural,
muddy or home-grown. The nation fell in love with all that
was packaged and processed – food was now bright, plastic
and quick. Metal aliens laughed heartily from the television
set, singing the wonders of powdered potatoes. In the time
it took to get the fork out of the garden shed, a fluffy dollop
of mashed nothingness was ready to be served. It was the
era of Dairylea cheese triangles, Angel Delight, Fray Bentos
tinned meat pies, cocktail sausages, Vesta's powdered
prawn curry and Mothers Pride. Honey monsters, manic
tigers and squawking cockerels invaded the breakfast tables
of the land, and prawn cocktails reigned supreme as the
height of culinary sophistication

I was never part of this food revolution, however. My
parents and grandparents grew vegetables and cooked from
raw ingredients. Porridge for breakfast, with a swirl of
golden syrup and a spoonful of malt extract. One foray into
the world of convenience food was the purchase of Ready
Brek. Lovely translucent melt-in-the-mouth flakes, tasting
exquisitely bland. What a treat! Of course, hunger kicked in
an hour later and that promised warm, rosy halo never
materialized.

The next-door neighbours were better at keeping the
faith. Four extremely fussy children, each of whom
demanded a different evening meal. All that was actually

required was knowing which Heinz tins to open, heat and spill on to slices of toast slavered with margarine – baked beans in tomato sauce; baked beans with sausage in tomato sauce; spaghetti hoops in tomato sauce; or alphabet spaghetti in tomato sauce. Delicious, it seems, with lashings of ketchup.

I adored fresh tomatoes, and watched this sacrilegious violence against my favourite food with indignation. The love of that juicy little fruit goes back to my grandfather's greenhouse. Built of abandoned window frames and odd pieces of wood, with a coal burner in the middle, this haven was suffused with the sweet, rich smell of warm tomatoes growing on the vine, sown from the seeds of those my grandfather had eaten and most enjoyed. To this day the smell of warm, ripe tomatoes transports me back to childhood days, and prompts a favourite lunch of a freshly plucked tomato, a freshly pulled lettuce and a freshly picked cucumber.

But food was not always so idyllic at my grandparents' house. I remember once refusing to eat tripe – well, please. Cooked in milk, there it sat on the plate looking every bit like the cow's stomach it was. With no intention of adding it to my stomach I sat stoically, lips sealed, for what seemed like an eternity, hoping it might disappear. Magically, it did. Suddenly, like a knight in shining overalls, my grandfather came in from the garden and, after recovering from his astonishment at my blatant demonstration of bad taste, poured half a bottle of Sarson's malt vinegar on to the tripe's quivering surfaces, and greedily slurped it off the plate. So much lip-smacking, so many grunts of satisfaction: I felt a slight twinge of regret at missing out on what was, for him at least, a delicious treat.

Later, and with the confidence of a real 'foodie', I entered a competition in a national newspaper asking children to describe their school lunches. At long last, a chance to vent my disgust at the quality of school food: at the lumpy custard and gloopy gravy, the gelatinous porridge and the spawn-like tapioca pudding, the over-cooked vegetables and undercooked eggs, the teeth-crushingly stale bread and leaden slices of cake. Disastrously, I won first prize. A shaming dressing-down from the headmistress ensued, as did a grovelling letter of apology to the school cook. All culinary pretensions were shattered.

A Food Lover's Treasury has given me the unexpected opportunity to do a little better second time around. I hope that readers will find this book appetizing, amusing and enlightening in equal portions. From Shelley's plea that we avoid meat and enjoy the pleasures of fruit and vegetables to Cobbett's celebration of the roasted English sirloin, there is, I hope, something to satisfy every taste bud.

My decision to follow Shelley's model sparked a determination to learn to cook properly. Since then, life has included many culinary experiments – several of which have found their way into my dogs' bellies or on to the bird table, or into the stomachs of my most underfed and least discerning friends. Getting over the continual disappointment that my food did not look anything like the magnificently alluring pictures in my cookbooks took a long time. Deciding to buy cookbooks without photographs to distract and dishearten was a good start. Eventually I learnt the tricks of cooking pastry, bread and sponge cake – those frustratingly difficult victuals that seem to require good karma as well as the right ingredients, the right oven and the right amount of kneading, stirring and rolling. And what a delight to discover how easy choux pastry is. Yes it is, really – and impressive to boot.

Today, cooking is a pleasure, even when my daughter looks at my offerings as though I have deliberately set out to poison her. I still have the odd moment when things end up in the bin or are thrown out of the kitchen window in a particularly colourful strop. But there are not many dishes nowadays that I would not have a go at, unless the recipe calls for sweet corn. Ugh. A peculiar little veg, and way too yellow. And who pulls it off the cob, anyway? It is far better cooked in its original state, smothered in butter and black pepper, and gnawed with gusto (so not the food for a first date). But at least I'm not scared of it. Julie has a strange fear of beetroot. In fact, she once inched her way past the cooker on which I was steaming a pan full of raw beetroot because to her horror one of the roots was hanging, tendril-like, from under the lid. I can only imagine that she feared it would climb out, chase her around the kitchen and eventually strangle her in a scene reminiscent of *The Day of the Triffids*. I've met many who object to the way in which beetroot seeps into the rest of any dish, turning everything violent purple; but to be spooked by a vegetable is perhaps a bit excessive. She is marginally outshone, however, by Smollett's Mrs Grizzle, who finds even the humble peach potentially life-threatening.

Collecting the quotations for this book has revealed a similarly intriguing range of approaches to the subject of food. Many of the extracts are hilariously funny: read Clive James's description of a typical Australian Christmas lunch. Some are surprisingly finger-wagging, as in the case of Samuel Johnson's diatribe against cucumbers. Others, such as Solzhenitsyn's account of semi-starvation in the Soviet Gulag, are simply tragic. And a select few are downright bizarre: take a look at Jerome K. Jerome's three men in a boat discussing whether or not to put a dead rat into their stew. In the process of discovering such tasty literary morsels, we came to appreciate the especially distinguished contribution made by certain writers. Charles Dickens, for example, writes so richly and copiously about food that it became incredibly difficult to decide which of his many wonderful passages to leave off our menu. Smollett was an equally juicy if more surprising source, witty and observant by turns, and offering an unparalleled insight into eighteenth-century attitudes to food. Our selection, however, extends far wider than their colourful prose – *A Food Lover's Treasury* is intended to satisfy all tastes. We hope you enjoy it and find something to tantalise and entice on every page. *Bon appetit*!

Lynda Murphy

I. FOOD PHILOSOPHY

'Of food you can talk on and on'

Food is a subject of conversation more spiritually refreshing even than the weather, for the number of possible remarks about the weather is limited, whereas of food you can talk on and on and on. Moreover, no heat of controversy is induced by mention of the atmospheric conditions (seeing that we are all agreed as to what is a good day and what is a bad one), and where there can be no controversy there can be no intimacy in agreement. But tastes in food differ so sharply (as has been well said in Latin and, I believe, also in French) that a pronounced agreement in them is of all bonds of union the most intimate. Thus, if a man hates tapioca pudding he is a good fellow and my friend.

A.A. Milne, 'Lunch' (1934).

His life was chiefly made up of dinners, of journeys to and from dinners, of talks about past dinners, and of speculations upon future dinners. He was an expert on salads as well as side-dishes and would discuss the art of salad-making with the utmost frankness, even laying down certain basic laws on the subject, but he was not an authority on any meal except dinner.

H. Pearson, *The Smith of Smiths* (1934).

The man who doesn't like oysters, the woman who cannot abide sardines. We know the type. For food, we are told, is the staple of life. In later life it becomes one of our rarest enjoyments. But it carries with it the germs of external as well as internal disorders; it carries with it the seeds of quarrels, violence, and misunderstanding. It is not a thing of which to think lightly, as of daily recurrence. It is a thing about which you must soberly think. Sit down and think. But be careful not to think too much.

Harold Nicolson, 'Food' (1942).

'I mind my belly very studiously'

Claude's mother was not discriminating about preachers. She believed them all chosen and sanctified, and was never happier than when she had one in the house to cook for and wait upon. She made young Mr Weldon so comfortable that he remained under her roof for several weeks, occupying the spare room, where he spent the mornings in study and meditation. He appeared regularly at mealtime to ask a blessing upon the food and to sit with devout, downcast eyes while the chicken was being dismembered. His top-shaped head hung a little to one side, the thin hair was parted precisely over his high forehead and brushed in little ripples. He was soft-spoken and apologetic in manner and took up as little room as possible. His meekness amused Mr Wheeler, who liked to ply him with food and never failed to ask him gravely 'what part of the chicken he would prefer,' in order to hear him murmur, 'A little of the white meat, if you please.'

Willa Cather, *One of Ours* (1922).

Sister Josephine knew that the Bishop, like all holy men of the cloth, had renounced the pleasures of the flesh, but she knew that nonetheless he would expect to be given exquisite food just so that he could demonstrate his indifference to it.

Michèle Roberts, 'The Bishop's Lunch' (1993).

In the middle of a pleasantly sunny little room – 'it is now Priscilla's boudoir,' Mr. Wimbush remarked parenthetically – stood a small circular table of mahogany. Crystal, porcelain, and silver, – all the shining apparatus of an elegant meal – were mirrored in its polished depths. The carcase of a cold chicken, a bowl of fruit, a great ham, deeply gashed to its heart of tenderest white and pink, the brown cannon ball of a cold plum-pudding, a slender Hock bottle, and a decanter of claret jostled one another for a place on this festive board. And round the table sat the three sisters, the three lovely Lapiths – eating!

At George's sudden entrance they had all looked towards the door, and now they sat, petrified by the same astonishment which kept George fixed and staring. Georgiana, who sat immediately facing the door, gazed at him with dark, enormous eyes. Between the thumb and forefinger of her right hand she was holding a drumstick of the dismembered chicken; her little finger, elegantly crooked, stood apart from the rest of her hand. Her mouth was open, but the drumstick had never reached its destination; it remained, suspended, frozen, in mid-air. The other two sisters had turned round to look at the intruder. Caroline still grasped her knife and fork; Emmeline's fingers were round the stem of her claret glass. For what seemed a very long time, George and the three sisters stared at one another in silence. They were a group of statues. Then suddenly there was movement. Georgiana dropped her chicken bone, Caroline's knife and fork clattered on her plate. The movement propagated itself, grew more decisive; Emmeline sprang to her feet, uttering a cry. The wave of panic reached George; he turned and, mumbling something unintelligible as he went, rushed out of the room and down the winding stairs. He came to a standstill in the hall, and there, all by himself in the quiet house, he began to laugh.

At luncheon it was noticed that the sisters ate a little more than usual. Georgiana toyed with some French beans and a spoonful of calves'-foot jelly. 'I feel a little stronger to-day,' she said to Lord Timpany, when he congratulated her on this increase of appetite; 'a little more material,' she added, with a nervous laugh. Looking up, she caught George's eye; a blush suffused her cheeks and she looked hastily away.

In the garden that afternoon they found themselves for a moment alone. 'You won't tell anyone, George? Promise you won't tell anyone,' she implored. 'It would make us look so ridiculous. And besides, eating *is* unspiritual, isn't it?'

Aldous Huxley, *Crome Yellow* (1921).

It is not positively affirmed that you shall not have a taste of the exciting, perhaps towards the middle and close of the meal, but it is resolved that the first dish set upon the table shall be one that a Catholic – ay, even an Anglo-Catholic – might eat on Good Friday in Passion Week: it shall be cold lentils and vinegar without oil; it shall be unleavened bread with bitter herbs, and no roast lamb.

Charlotte Brontë, *Shirley* (1849).

There was the problem of Professor Godbole and his food, and of Professor Godbole and other people's food – two problems, not one problem. The Professor was a very strict Hindu – he would take tea, fruit, soda-water and sweets, whoever cooked them, and vegetables and rice if cooked by a Braham; but not meat, not cakes lest they contained eggs, and he would not allow anyone else to eat beef: a slice of beef upon a distant plate would wreck his happiness. •

E.M. Forster, *A Passage to India* (1924).

There was, for example, her stomach. She was used to certain dishes, and she had a strong conviction that she could not possibly eat anything else. There must be a lemonade and a tomato sandwich later in the morning, then a light lunch with a stuffed tomato. Not only did she require food from a selection of a dozen dishes, but in addition this food must be prepared in just a certain way. One of the most annoying half hours of the first fortnight occurred in Los Angeles, when an unhappy waiter brought her a tomato stuffed with chicken salad instead of celery.

F. Scott Fitzgerald, *The Beautiful and the Damned* (1922).

Some people have a foolish way of not minding, or pretending not to mind, what they eat. For my part, I mind my belly very studiously, and very carefully; for I look upon it, that he who does not mind his belly will hardly mind anything else.

James Boswell, *Life of Johnson* (1791).

'Life,' said Emerson, 'consists in what a man is thinking all day.' If that be so, then my life is nothing but a big intestine. I not only think about food all day, but I dream about it at night.

Henry Miller, *Tropic of Cancer* (1963).

'May I have some bread?' she asked.

The grossest indecency would not have fallen on the ears of those three women with such a shock. Not one of them had eaten bread for ten years. Even Beatrice, greedy as she was, drew the line there. Frank, the good hostess, recovered herself first.

'Of course, darling,' she said and turning to the butler asked him to bring some.

'And some butter,' said Lena in that pleasant way of hers.

'I don't know if there's any in the house,' said Frank, 'but I'll enquire. There may be some in the kitchen.'

'I adore bread and butter, don't you?' said Lena, turning to Beatrice.

Beatrice gave a sickly smile and an evasive reply. The butler brought a long crisp roll of French bread. Lena slit it in two and plastered it with the butter which was miraculously produced. The grilled sole was served.

'We eat very simply here,' said Frank. 'I hope you won't mind.'

'Oh, no, I like my food very plain,' said Lena as she took some butter and spread it over her fish. 'As long as I can have bread and butter and potatoes and cream I'm quite happy.'

The three friends exchanged a glance. Frank's great sallow face sagged a little and she looked with distaste at the dry, insipid sole on her plate. Beatrice came to the rescue.

'It's such a bore, we can't get cream here,' she said. 'It's one of the things one has to do without on the Riviera.'

'What a pity,' said Lena.

The rest of the luncheon consisted of lamb cutlets, with the fat carefully removed so that Beatrice should not be led astray, and spinach boiled in water, with stewed pears to end up with. Lena tasted her pears and gave the butler a look of enquiry. That resourceful man understood her at once and though powdered sugar had never been served at that table before handed her without a moment's hesitation a bowl of it. She helped herself liberally. The other three pretended not to notice. Coffee was served and Lena took three lumps of sugar in hers.

'You have a very sweet tooth,' said Arrow in a tone which she struggled to keep friendly.

'We think saccharine so much more sweetening,' said Frank as she put a tiny tablet of it into her coffee.

'Disgusting stuff,' said Lena.

Beatrice's mouth drooped at the corners, and she gave the lump sugar a yearning look.

'Beatrice,' boomed Frank sternly.

Beatrice stifled a sigh, and reached for the saccharine.

W. Somerset Maugham, 'The Three Fat Women of Antibes' (1951).

She purchased Culpepper's midwifery, which, with that sagacious performance dignified with Aristotle's name, she studied with indefatigable care, and diligently perused the *Compleat House-wife*, together with Quincy's dispensatory, culling every jelly, marmalade and conserve which these authors recommend as either salutary or toothsome, for the benefit and comfort of her sister-in-law, during her gestation. She restricted her from eating roots, pot-herbs, fruit, and all sorts of vegetables; and one day when Mrs Pickle had plucked a peach with her own hand, and was in the very act of putting it between her teeth, Mrs Grizzle perceived the rash attempt, and running up to her, fell upon her knees in the garden intreating her, with tears in her eyes, to resist such a pernicious appetite.

Tobias Smollett, *The Adventure of Peregrine Pickle* (1751).

He had a laudable care for his own bodily health – kept very early hours, regularly took a walk before breakfast, was vastly particular about warm and dry clothing, had never been known to preach a sermon without previously swallowing a raw egg – albeit he was gifted with good lungs and a powerful voice, – and was, generally, extremely particular about what he ate and drank, though by no means abstemious, and having a mode of dietary peculiar to himself, – being a great despiser of tea and such slops, and a patron of malt liquors, bacon and eggs, ham, hung beef, and other strong meats, which agreed well enough with his digestive organs, and therefore were maintained by him to be good and wholesome for everybody, and confidently recommended to the most delicate convales-cents or dyspeptics, who, if they failed to derive the promised benefit from his prescriptions, were told it was because they had not persevered, and if they complained of inconvenient results there from, were assured it was all fancy.

Anne Brontë, *The Tenant of Wildfell Hall* (1848).

As I intend to sail in the morning some hands were employ'd picking of Sellery to take to sea with us, this is found here in great plenty and I have caused it to be boild with Portable Soup and Oatmeal every morning for the Peoples breakfast, and this I design to continue as long as it will last or any is to be got, because I look upon it to be very wholesome and a great Antiscorbutick.

Captain Cook, diary entry Saturday 28 October, 1769.

Wouldn't it be awful if spinach hain't really healthful after all th' trouble it takes t'git the sand out of it?

'Kin' Hubbard, *Abe Martin's Wisecracks* (1930).

Everything we did proceeded according to schedule and in line with an over-all plan. She was very strong, naturally, on toilet-training, and everything in our life was directed toward the after-breakfast session on 'the throne.' Our whole diet – not to speak of the morning orange juice with castor oil in it that was brought to us on the slightest pretext of 'paleness' – was centred around this levee. We had prunes every day for breakfast, and corn-meal mush. Wheatena, or farina, which I had to eat plain, since by some medical whim it had been decided that milk was bad for me. The rest of our day's menu consisted of parsnips, turnips, rutabagas, carrots, boiled potatoes, boiled cabbage, onions, Swiss chard, kale, and so on; most green vegetables, apparently, were too dear to be appropriate for us, though I think that, beyond this, the family had a sort of moral affinity with the root vegetable, stemming, perhaps, from everything fibrous, tenacious, watery, and knobbly in the Irish peasant stock. Our deserts were rice pudding, farina pudding, over-cooked custard with little air-holes in it, prunes, stewed red plums, rhubarb, stewed pears, stewed dried peaches. We must have had meat, but I have only the most indistinct recollection of pale lamb stews in which the carrots outnumbered the pieces of white, fatty meat and bone and gristle; certainly we did not have steak or roasts or turkey or fried chicken, but perhaps an occasional boiled fowl was served to us with its vegetable (for I do remember the neck, shrunken in its collar of puckered skin, coming to me as my portion, and the fact that if you sucked on it, you could draw out the edible white cord), and doubt-less there was meat loaf and beef stew. There was no ice-cream, cake, pie, or butter, but on rare mornings we had johnnycake or large woolly pancakes with Karo syrup.

We were not allowed to leave the table until every morsel was finished, and I used to sit through half a dark winter afternoon staring at the cold carrots on my plate, until, dur-ing one short snowy period, I found that I could throw them out of the back window if I raised it very quietly.

Mary McCarthy, *Memories of a Catholic Girlhood* (1957).

Let us clearly perceive that three meals a day all one's life not only give in themselves a constantly rewarded satisfac-tion, but provide the necessary foundation for all other satis-factions. Taking food and drink is a great enjoyment for healthy people, and those who do not enjoy eating seldom have much capacity for enjoyment or usefulness of any sort.

Charles W. Eliot, *The Happy Life* (1896).

Love and business and family and religion and art and patriotism are nothing but shadows of words when a man's starving.

O. Henry, 'Cupid à la carte', *Heart of the West* (1907).

'The phantasm of appetite'

'What a breakfast I *shall* eat!' thought Jack Abbott, as he turned into Middle Temple Lane, towards the chambers of his old friend and tutor Goodall. 'How I shall swill the tea! how cram down the rolls (especially the inside bits)! how apologise for "one cup more!" – But Goodall is an excellent fellow – he won't mind. To be sure I'm rather late. The rolls, I'm afraid, will be cold, or double baked; but anything will be delicious. If I met a baker, I could eat his basket.'

Jack Abbott was a good-hearted follow, who had walked that morning from Hendon, to breakfast with his old friend by appointment . . . Well, Jack Abbott has arrived at the door of his friend's room. He knocks; and it is opened by Goodall himself, a thin grizzled personage, in an old great-coat instead of a gown, with lanthorn-jaws, shaggy eyebrows and a most bland and benevolent expression of countenance . . .

Unfortunately for the hero of our story, this angel of sixty-five, unshaved, and with stockings down at heel, had a memory which could not recollect what had been told him six hours before, much less six days. Accordingly he had finished his breakfast, and given his cat the remaining drop of milk long before his (in every sense of the word) pupil presented himself within his threshold . . .

'Come in, pray; come in and sit down, and let's hear all about the good lady your mother, and how you all get on . . .'

'Capitally well, sir (*looking at the breakfast-table*). I'm quite rejoiced to see that the breakfast-cloth is not removed; for I'm horribly late, and fear I must have put you out; but don't you take any trouble, my good sir. The kettle, I see, is still singing on the hob. I'll cut myself a piece of bread and butter immediately; and you'll let me scramble beside you as I used to do, and look at a book, and talk with my mouth full.'

Goodall. 'Ay, ay; what! You have come to breakfast, have you, my kind boy? that is very good of you, very good indeed. Let me see – let me see – my laundress has never been here this morning, but you won't mind my serving you myself – I have everything at hand.'

Abbott (apart, and sighing with a smile). 'He has forgotten all about the invitation! Thank ye, my dear sir, thank ye – I would apologise, only I know you wouldn't like it; and to say the truth, I'm very hungry – hungry as a hunter – I've come all the way from Hendon.'

'Bless me! have you, indeed? and from Wendover too? Why, that is a very long way, isn't it?' . . .

'I beg pardon,' interrupted Jack, who in a fury of hunger and thirst, was pouring out what tea he could find in the pot, and anxiously looking for the bread; 'I can do very well with this – at any rate to begin with.'

'Just so, sir,' balmily returned Goodall. 'Well, sir, but I am sorry to see – eh, I really fear – certainly the cat – eh – what are we to do for milk? I'm afraid I must make you wait till I step out for some; for this laundress, when once she—'

'Don't stir, I beg you,' ejaculated our hero; 'don't think of it, my dear sir. I can do very well without milk – I can indeed – I *often* do without milk.'

This was said out of an intensity of a sense to the contrary; but Jack was anxious to make the old gentleman easy.

'Well,' quoth Goodall, 'I have met with such instances, to be sure; and very lucky it is, Mr – a – John – James I should say – that you do not care for milk; though I confess for my part, I cannot do without it. But, bless me! heyday! Well, if the sugar-basin, dear me, is not empty. Bless my soul! I'll go instantly – it is but as far as Fleet Street – and my hat, I think, must be under those pamphlets.'

'Don't think of such a thing, pray, dear sir,' cried Jack, half leaping from his chair, and tenderly laying his hand on his arm. 'You may think it odd; but sugar, I can assure you, is a good thing I don't *at all* care for. Do you know, my dear Mr Goodall, I have often had serious thoughts of leaving off sugar, owing to the slave trade?'

'Why that, indeed —'

'Yes, sir; and probably I should have done it, had not so many excellent men, yourself among them, thought it fit to continue the practice, no doubt after the greatest reflection. However, what with these perhaps foolish doubts, and the indifference of my palate to sweets, sugar is a mere drug to me, sir – a mere drug.'

'Well, but—'

'Nay, dear sir, you will distress me if you say another word upon the matter – you will indeed; see how I drink. (And here Jack made as if he took a hasty gulp of his milkless and sugarless water.) 'The bread, my dear sir – the bread is all I require; just that piece which you were going to take up. You remember how I used to stuff bread, and fill the book I was reading with crumbs? I dare say the old Euripides is bulging out with them now.'

'Well, sir – ah – em – ah – well, indeed, you're very good, and, I'm sure, very temperate; but dear me – well, this laundress of mine – I must certainly get rid of her thieving – rheumatism, I should say; but *butter!* I vow I do not—'

'*Butter!*' interrupted our hero, in the tone of the greatest scorn. 'Why, I haven't eaten *butter* I don't know when. Not a step, sir, not a step. And now let me tell you I must make haste, for I've got to lunch with my lawyer, and he'll expect me to eat something; and in fact I'm so anxious, and feel so hurried, that now I have eaten a good piece of my hunk, I must be off, my good sir – I must indeed.'

To say the truth, Jack's hunk was a good three days old, if an hour; and so hard, that even his hunger and fine teeth could not find it in the hearts of them to relish it with the cold slop; so he had made up his mind to seek the nearest coffee-house as fast as possible, and there have the heartiest and most luxurious breakfast that could make amends for his disappointment . . .

Being once more out of doors, our hero rushes back like a tiger into Fleet Street, and plunges into the first coffee-house in sight.

'Waiter!'

'*Yessir.*'

'Breakfast immediately. Tea, black and green, and all that.'

'*Yessir*. Eggs and toast, sir?'

'By all means.'

'*Yessir*. Any ham sir?'

'Just so, and instantly.'

'*Yessir*. Cold fowl sir?'

'Precisely; and no delay.'

'*Yessir*. Anchovy, perhaps, sir?'

'By all – eh? – no, I don't care for anchovy – but pray bring what you like; and above all, make haste, my good fellow – no delay – I'm as hungry as the devil.'

Leigh Hunt, 'Jack Abbott's Breakfast' (1847).

Poor men, and those that fast often, have much more pleasure in eating than rich men, and gluttons, that always feed before their stomachs are empty of their last meat and call for more; for by that means they rob themselves of that pleasure that hunger brings to poor men.

Izaak Walton, *The Compleat Angler* (1653).

'Is there anything you can fancy that you would like to eat?' I once said to an old labouring man, who was in his last illness, and who had refused all the food his wife had offered him. 'No,' he answered, 'I've never been used to nothing but

common victual, and I can't eat that.' Experience had bred no
fancies in him that could raise the phantasm of appetite.

George Eliot, *Silas Marner* (1861).

Lord D— placed before me a most magnificent breakfast. It
was really so; but in my eyes it seemed trebly magnificent – from
being the first regular meal, the first 'good man's table', that I had
sat down to for months. Strange to say, however, I could scarcely
eat any thing. On the day when I first received my 10l. bank-
note, I had gone to a baker's shop and bought a couple of rolls:
this very shop I had two months or six weeks before surveyed
with an eagerness of desire which it was almost humiliating to
me to recollect. I remember the story about Otway; and feared
that there might be danger in eating too rapidly. But I had no
need for alarm, my appetite was quite sunk, and I became sick
before I had eaten half of what I had bought. This effect from
eating what approached to a meal, I continued to feel for weeks:
or, when I did not experience any nausea, part of what I ate was
rejected, sometimes with acidity, sometimes immediately, and
without any acidity. On the present occasion, at Lord D—'s
table, I found myself not all better than usual: and in the midst of
luxuries, I had no appetite.

Thomas de Quincey, *Confessions of an English Opium Eater* (1821).

'Perhaps you'd care for something to eat?' said the
Mathemagician, offering each of them a heaped bowlful.

'Yes, sir,' said Milo, who was beside himself with hunger.

'Thank you,' added Tock.

The Humbug made no reply, for he was already too busy eating, and in a moment the three of them had finished absolutely
everything they'd been given.

'Please have another portion,' said the Mathemagician, filling
their bowls once more; and as quickly as they'd finished the first
one the second was emptied too.

'Don't stop now,' he insisted, serving them again,
and again,
and again,
and again,
and again.

'How very strange,' thought Milo as he finished his seventh helping. 'Each one I eat makes me a little hungrier than that one before.'

'Do have some more,' suggested the Mathemagician, and they continued to eat just as fast as he filled the plates.

After Milo had eaten nine portions, Tock eleven, and the Humbug, without once stopping to look up, twenty-three, the Mathemagician blew his whistle for the second time and immediately the pot was removed and the miners returned to work.

'U-g-g-g-h-h-h,' gasped the bug, suddenly realising that he was twenty-three times hungrier than when he started, 'I think I'm starving.'

'Me, too,' complained Milo, whose stomach felt as empty as he could ever remember; 'and I ate so much.'

'Yes, it was delicious, wasn't it?' agreed the pleased Dodecahedron, wiping the gravy from several of his mouths. 'It's the speciality of the kingdom – subtraction stew.'

'I have more of an appetite than when I began,' said Tock, leaning weakly against one of the larger rocks.

'Certainly,' replied the Mathemagician; 'what did you expect? The more you eat, the hungrier you get. Everyone knows that.'

'They do?' said Milo doubtfully, 'Then how do you ever get enough?'

'Enough?' he said impatiently. 'Here in Digitopolis we have our meals when we're full and eat until we're hungry. That way, when you don't have anything at all, you have more than enough. It's a very economical system. You must have been quite stuffed to eat so much.'

Norton Juster, *The Phantom Tollbooth* (1962).

2. TASTE

'The pleasures of taste'

The best and most wholesome feeding is upon one dish and no more and the same plain and simple: for surely this huddling of many meats one upon another of divers tastes is pestiferous. But sundry sauces are more dangerous than that.

Pliny, *Historia Naturalis* (AD 77).

The pleasures of taste to be derived from a dinner of potatoes, beans, peas, turnips, lettice, with a dessert of apples, gooseberries, strawberries, currants, raspberries, and in winter, oranges, apples and pears, is far greater than is supposed.

Percy Bysshe Shelley, 'A Vindication of Natural Diet' (1813).

Talking of Pleasure, this moment I was writing with one hand, and with thither holding to my Mouth a Nectarine – good God how fine. It went down soft pulpy, slushy, oozy – all its delicious embonpoint melted down my throat like a large Beatified Strawberry.

John Keats, letter to Charles Wentworth Dilke,
22 September, 1818.

It was a heavenly place for a boy, that farm of my uncle John's. The house was a double log one, with a spacious floor (roofed in) connecting it with the kitchen. In the summer the table was set in the middle of that shady and breezy floor, and the sumptuous meals – well, it makes me cry to think of them. Fried chicken, roast pig; wild and tame turkeys, ducks and

geese, venison just killed, squirrels, rabbits, pheasants, partridges, prairie-chickens; biscuits, hot batter cakes, hot buckwheat cakes, hot 'wheat bread',' hot rolls, hot corn pone; fresh
corn boiled on the ear, succotash, butter-beans, string beans,
tomatoes, peas, Irish potatoes, sweet potatoes; buttermilk,
sweet milk, 'clabber'; watermelons, muskmelons, cantaloupes
– all fresh from the garden; apple pie, peach pie, pumpkin pie,
apple dumplings, peach cobbler – I can't remember the rest.

Mark Twain, *Autobiography* (1925).

Talk of joy: there may be things better than beef stew and
baked potatoes and home-made bread – there may be.

David Grayson, *Adventures in Contentment* (1907).

You know Dick Hopkins, the swearing scullion of Caius?
This fellow, by industry and agility, has thrust himself into the
important situations (no sinecures, believe me) of cook to
Trinity Hall and Caius College: and the generous creature has
contrived, with the greatest delicacy imaginable, to send me a
present of Cambridge brawn . . . At first I thought of declining
the present; but Richard knew my blind side when he pitched
upon brawn. 'Tis of all my hobbies the supreme in the eating
way. He might have sent sops from the pan, skimmings, crumpets, chips, hog's lard, the tender brown tops of asparagus,
fugitive livers, runaway gizzards of fowls, the eyes of martyred
pigs, tender effusions of laxative woodcocks, the red spawn of
lobsters, leveret's ears and such pretty filchings common to
cooks; but these had been ordinary presents, the every-day
courtesies of dish-washers to their sweet-hearts. Brawn was a
noble picture of the choice old Italian masters. Its gusto is of
that hidden sort. As Wordsworth sings of a modest poet – 'you
must love him, ere to you he will seem worthy of your love'; so
brawn, you must taste it ere to you it will seem to have any
taste at all. But 'tis nuts to the adept: those what will send out

their tongue and feelers to find it out. It will be wooed, and not unsought be won. Now, ham-essence, lobsters, turtle, such popular minions, absolutely *court you*, lay themselves out to strike you at first smack, like one of David's pictures compared with the plain russet-coated wealth of a Titian or a Correggio, as I illustrated above. Such are the obvious glaring heathen virtues of a corporation dinner, compared with the reserved collegiate worth of brawn.

Charles Lamb, letter to Thomas Manning, 24 February, 1804.

'There is no such passion in human nature as the passion for gravy among commercial gentlemen. It's nothing to say a joint won't yield – a whole animal wouldn't yield – the amount of gravy they expect at dinner. And what I have undergone in consequence,' cried Mrs Todgers, raising her eyes and shaking her head, 'no-one would believe!'

Charles Dickens, *Martin Chuzzlewit* (1844).

Topaz had boiled half the ham. She said it would go further if we didn't cut it until it was quite cold, but Thomas insisted – he had been very possessive about that ham. We all fanned it with newspapers until the last moment. It was wonderful, of course – ham with mustard is a meal of glory.

Dodie Smith, *I Capture the Castle* (1949).

When I lifted the lid we were intoxicated by a dizzying heady aroma. It smelt of richness, warmth, celebration, elegance, the triumph of gluttony! I had stewed this precious thing from Orangini for two hours over a low heat, shut tightly in with slices of ham, fillet of beef, with some good white wine, a vegetable stock and rashers of bacon. My Georges ate it slowly, gravely, silently – and went on thanking me for it all day. There's nothing more sincere than the gratitude of a satisfied palate!

Liane de Pougy, diary entry 25 December, 1924.

A packet of Jaffas was loaded like a cluster bomb with about fifty globular lollies the size of ordinary marbles. The Jaffa had a dark chocolate core and a brittle orange candy coat: in cross section it looked rather like the planet Earth. It presented two alternative ways of being eaten, each with its allure. You could fondle the Jaffa on the tongue until your saliva ate its way through the casing, whereupon the taste of chocolate would invade your mouth with a sublime, majestic inevitability. Or you could bite straight through and submit the interior of your head to a stunning explosion of flavour.

Clive James, *Unreliable Memoirs* (1980).

Mmmmmmmmmmmmmmmmm. These are nice. Little Roquefort cheese morsels rolled in crushed nuts. Very tasty. Very subtle. It's the way the dry sackiness of the nuts tiptoes up against the dour savour of the cheese that is so nice, so subtle.

Tom Wolfe, *Radical Chic* (1970).

How I do love eating. Such bliss: the taste of salt and hot olive oil coating this cloud of deep-fried egg white, the lightest of fritters, melting inside with Gruyère, each mouthful sliding over my tongue and down my throat, filling me up deep inside until at long last I am sated and can finally stop. Heavy with pleasure. Food like a sack of gold in my belly. My barn of harvest grain; my treasure store against the years of famine. I'll never starve again, for there is always more, as much as I want.

Michèle Roberts, 'The Cookery Lesson' (2001).

The Governor . . . looked forward with great impatience to nightfall and meal-time; and even though time seemed to him to be standing still, at length the long wished of moment arrived, and they gave him for his supper a hash of beef and onions and some boiled calves' feet, rather stale from keeping. But he fell to it all with more pleasure than if he had been given

Milan game, Roman pheasants, Sorrento veal, Moron partridges, or Lavajos geese; and during his supper he turned to the doctor and said: 'Look here, Master Doctor, you needn't trouble in future to give me choice things and delicate dainties, for that would mean wrenching my stomach off its hinges. It's used to kid, beef, bacon, salt meat, turnips and onions, and if it's given palace food by chance, it takes it with queasiness and sometimes with loathing. I'd like the butler to bring me mixed stews – as they call them; and the stronger they are the higher they smell. He can shove in anything he likes so long as it's good to eat, and I'll thank him for it, and pay him one day.

Miguel de Cervantes, *Don Quixote* (1604).

At first he had amorously deceived himself into liking her experiments with food – the one medium in which she could express imagination – but now he wanted only his round of favourite dishes: steak, roast beef, boiled pig's-feet, oatmeal, baked apples. Because at some more flexible period he had advanced from oranges to grape-fruit he considered himself an epicure.

Sinclair Lewis, *Main Street* (1920).

The aspect of those monumental dishes of macaroni was worthy of the quivers of admiration they evoked. The burnished gold of the crusts, the fragrance of sugar and cinnamon they exuded, were but preludes to the delights released from the interior when the knife broke the crust; first came a spice-laden haze, then chicken livers, hard boiled eggs, sliced ham, chicken and truffles in masses of piping hot, glistening macaroni, to which the meat juice gave an exquisite hue of suede.

Guiseppe di Lampedusa, *The Leopard* (1958).

During that summer he ate for the first time a salad with a lemon and oil dressing and, at breakfast, yoghurt – a glamorous substance he knew only from a James Bond novel. His hard-pressed father's cooking and the pie-and-chips regime of his student days could not have prepared him for the strange vegetables – the aubergines, green and red peppers, courgettes and mangetouts – that came regularly before him. He was surprised, even a little put out, on his first visit when Violet served as a first course a bowl of under-cooked peas. He had to overcome an aversion, not to the taste as to the reputation of the garlic. Ruth giggled for minutes on end, until she had to leave the room, when he called a baguette a croissant. Early on, he made an impression on the Pontings by claiming never to have been abroad, except to Scotland to climb the three Munroes of the Knoydart peninsula. He encountered for the first time in his life muesli, olives, fresh black pepper, bread without butter, anchovies, undercooked lamb, cheese that was not cheddar, ratatouille, saucisson, bouillabaisse, entire meals without potatoes, and, most challenging of all, a fishy pink paste, tarama salata. Many of these items tasted only faintly repellent, and similar to each other in some indefinable way, but he was determined not to appear unsophisticated.

Ian McEwan, *On Chesil Beach* (2007).

'What do you like to eat?' Helga asked.

The question stopped him. He'd never really thought about it. Most things came from cans. Is that what she meant? 'I guess . . . I don't know. Everything, I guess.'

'Everything. That is good.'

'I like hot dogs,' he said. 'I like Prexy's.'

She turned to Franz. 'What is this Prexy's?'

'Hamburgers,' Franz said.

'I like milk.'

'*Ja*. Milk is good.' She rubbed her hands and smiled at Franz. 'I make something special for Friday.'

And so it began. At the end of the next practice session, Claude tugged the bell pull and Franz came in to watch him do his push-ups. After washing his hands, the boy followed him into the dining room. A full service had been set up at the head of the table. Claude was intimidated by the elaborate setup, the gleaming plates and silver.

'Sit,' Franz said.

'What is all this, how do I, which—'

'Relax, please. He wants you to learn this. There are different courses. It's very simple. Take the napkin from the ring and spread it over your lap. That's right. Now I will serve the soup.'

Franz ladled the pale green liquid. Claude sat perfectly still, watching the deft moves of the old man at his shoulder. The soup smelled good.

'Cream of asparagus. Use the outside spoon. And here is bread and butter. This is the butter knife. It stays on this little plate. Go ahead now.' Franz surprised him by going off into the kitchen through the swinging doors. After a moment, Claude heard the soft murmur of their voices. The clink of plates, a chair scraping.

He picked up the indicated spoon and took a sip of the soup. Claude had never tasted asparagus, never eaten a soup made from scratch, and was entirely unprepared for the warm, slow-motion explosion of please that now filled his head. (Asparagus soup was to become a lifelong favourite, although he would never find the equal to Helga's inspired ambrosial mixture of stock, tips, herbs, and cream. Nor would he know he was the beneficiary of her training in the lost royal Austro-Hungarian Empire.) He ate as if in a dream.

Franz appeared, to remove the shallow bowl and replace it with a plate bearing Wiener schnitzel adorned with a thin slice of lemon, potato dumplings in butter, and a glistening mélange of string beans and sliced red peppers. 'At a formal dinner,' he explained, 'each of these might be brought round the table, and of course you would not begin to eat until the host or hostess began.'

'Okay.'

Franz returned and Claude picked up his knife and fork. The dream continued – he barely heard the soft laughter from the kitchen, the chiming of the grandfather clock in the foyer, or the creak of the upholstered chair on which he sat. He was immersed in swirls of texture, colour, and taste. He ate slowly, sometimes closing his eyes.

Franz regarded the empty plate. Even the lemon slice was gone. 'Dessert,' he said, removing the plate and setting down a bowl of bananas and cream dusted with brown sugar. 'Two desserts.' A saucer of apple strudel, still warm from the oven. 'She is a good cook, Helga. Don't you think?'

He was speechless. He could only nod.

Frank Conroy, *Body and Soul* (1993).

They had 'It' on a plate. They had cut it into quarters and covered it with lovely custard. Mrs Williams pushed her hair-brush deep into her pinny pocket and thrust the pudding at him. She moved the bowl through the air with such speed that the spoon was left behind and clattered onto the cobble floor.

Mrs Williams stopped, but Fanny Drabble hissed: 'Leave alone.' She kicked the fallen spoon away and gave Oscar a fresh one. She was suddenly nervous of discovery.

Oscar took the spoon and ate standing up.

He could never have imagined such a lovely taste. He let it break apart, treasuring it in his mouth.

He looked up and saw the two mirrored smiles increase. Fanny Drabble tucked her chin into her neck. Oscar smiled too, almost sleepily, and he was just raising the spoon to his mouth in anticipation of more, and had actually got the second spoonful into his mouth when the door squeaked open behind him and Theophilus came striding across the cobbled floor.

He did not see this. He felt it. He felt the blow on the back of his head. His face leapt forward. The spoon hit his tooth. The spoon dropped to the floor. A large horny hand gripped the back of his head and another cupped beneath his mouth. He tried to swallow. There was a second blow. He spat what he could.

Theophilus acted as if his son were poisoned. He brought him to his scullery and made him drink salt water. He forced the glass hard against his mouth so it hurt. Oscar gagged and struggled. His father's eyes were wild. They did not see him. Oscar drank. He drank again. He drank until he vomited into the pig's swill. When this was done, Theophilus threw what remained of the pudding into the fire.

Oscar had never been hit before. He did not believe it.

His father made a speech. Oscar did not believe it.

His father said the pudding was the fruit of Satan.

But Oscar tasted the pudding. It did not taste like the fruit of Satan.

Peter Carey, *Oscar and Lucinda* (1988).

'Chief of this world's luxuries': fruit

Enter an unreflecting young gentleman who has bought an orange and must eat it immediately. He accordingly begins by peeling it, and is first made aware of the delicacy of his position by the gigglement of the two young ladies, and his doubt where he shall throw the peel. 'He is in for it,' however, and must proceed; so being unable to divide the orange into its segments, he ventures upon a great liquid bite, which resounds through the omnibus, and covers the lower part of his face with pip and drip. The young lady with the ringlets is right before him. The two other young ladies stuff their handkerchiefs into their mouths, and he into his own mouth the rest of the fruit, 'sloshy' and too big, with desperation in his heart, and the tears in his eyes. Never will he eat an orange again in an omnibus.

Leigh Hunt, 'The Inside of an Omnibus' (1876).

Oranges should be eaten in solitude and as a treat when one is feeling hungry. They are too messy and overwhelming to form part of an ordinary meal.

Iris Murdoch, *The Sea, The Sea* (1987).

When oranges came in, a curious proceeding was gone through. Miss Jenkyns did not like to cut the fruit; for, as she observed, the juice all ran out nobody knew where; sucking (only I think she used some more recondite word) was in fact the only way of enjoying oranges; but then there was the unpleasant association with a ceremony frequently gone through by little babies; and so, after dessert, in orange season, Miss Jenkyns and Miss Matty used to rise up, possess themselves each of an orange in silence, and withdraw to the privacy of their own rooms, to indulge in sucking oranges.

Elizabeth Gaskell, *Cranford* (1853).

Now you know what a grapefruit's like: the way it spurts juice down your shirt and keeps slipping out of your hand unless you hold it down with a fork or something, the way the flesh always sticks to those opaque membranes and then suddenly comes loose with half the pith attached, the way it always tastes sour yet makes you feel bad about piling sugar on the top of it. That's what a grapefruit's like, right? Now let me tell you about *this* grapefruit. Its flesh was pink for a start not yellow, and each segment had already been carefully freed from its clinging membrane. The fruit itself was anchored to the dish by some prong or fork through its bottom, so that I didn't need to hold it down or even touch it. I looked around for the sugar, but that was just out of habit. The taste seemed to come in two parts – a sort of awakening sharpness followed quickly by a wash of sweetness; and each of those little globules (which were about the size of tadpoles) seemed to burst separately in my mouth. That was the grapefruit of my dreams, I don't mind telling you.

Julian Barnes, *A History of the World in 10½ Chapters* (1989).

The whole party were assembled, excepting Frank Churchill, who was expected every moment from Richmond; and Mrs. Elton, in all her apparatus of happiness, her large bonnet and her basket, was very ready to lead the way in gathering, accepting, or talking – strawberries, and only strawberries, could now be thought or spoken of. – 'The best fruit in England – everybody's favourite – always wholesome. – These the finest beds and finest sorts. – Delightful to gather for one's self-the only way of really enjoying them. – Morning decidedly the best time – never tired – every sort good – hautboy infinitely superior – no comparison – the others hardly eatable – hautboys very scarce – Chili preferred – white wood finest flavour of all – price of strawberries in London – abundance about Bristol – Maple Grove – cultivation – beds when to be renewed – gardeners thinking exactly different – no general rule – gardeners never to be put out of their way – delicious fruit – only too rich to be eaten much of – inferior to cherries – currants more refreshing – only objection to gathering strawberries the stooping – glaring sun – tired to death – could bear it no longer – must go and sit in the shade.'

Jane Austen, *Emma* (1815).

'She brought some of those apples. I was obliged to eat them. It was against my principles, but I find that principles have no real force except when one is well fed.'

Mark Twain, *The Diary of Adam and Eve* (1893).

There are some fruits which awaken in me feelings deeper than appetite. When I contemplate the musky golden orb of the sugar-melon, or the green and brown seaweed marking of the tiger cantaloupe, the scales of the pineapple or the texture of figs and nectarines, the disposition of oranges and lemons on the tree or the feign-death coils of the old vine-serpent, I swell in unity with them, I ripen with the sugar-cane, the banana in flower.

Cyril Connolly, *The Unquiet Grave* (1944).

For three centimes I can eat, drink, and wash my face, all by the means of one of those slices of water-melon you display there on a little table.

Anatole France, *The Crime of Sylvestre Bonnard* (1881).

The true Southern watermelon is a boon apart, and not to be mentioned with commoner things. It is chief of this world's luxuries, king by the grace of God over all the fruits of the earth. When one has tasted it, he knows what the angels eat. It was not a Southern watermelon that Eve took; we know it because she repented.

Mark Twain, *Pudd'nhead Wilson* (1894).

Always eat grapes downwards – that is, always eat the best grape first; in this way there will be none better left on the bunch, and each grape will seem good down to the last. If you eat the other way, you will not have a good grape in the lot.

Samuel Butler, *The Notebooks of Samuel Butler* (1912).

There's no question but her tetchiness and most vulturous eating of the apricots are apparent signs of breeding.

John Webster, *The Duchess of Malfi* (1623).

I have always viewed with a proper amount of respect and abhorrence those penetrating spirits who are not susceptible to appearances. What is there to believe in except appearances? I have nearly always found that they are the only things worth enjoying at all, and if ever an innocent child lays its head upon my knee and begs for the truth of the matter, I shall tell it the story of my one and only nurse, who, knowing my horror of gooseberry jam, spread a coat of apricot over the top of the jam jar. As long as I believed it apricot I was happy, and learning wisdom, I contrived to eat the apricot and leave the gooseberry behind. 'So, you see, my little innocent creature,' I shall end. 'The great thing to learn in this life is to be content with appearances, and shun the vulgarities of the grocer and philosopher.'

Katherine Mansfield, 'Pension Seguin' (1913).

'Heavens! I was quite forgetting!' he cried suddenly. 'I have some wonderful raisins with me – you know, those seedless ones. Our new sutler has such first-rate things. I bought ten pounds. I always like sweet things. Will you have sóme? . . .' And Petya ran out to his Cossack in the passage and returned with baskets containing about five pounds of raisins. 'Help yourselves gentlemen, help yourselves!'

Leo Tolstoy, *War and Peace* (1869).

A fruit is a vegetable with looks and money. Plus, if you let fruit rot, it turns into wine, something Brussels sprouts never do.

P.J. O'Rourke, *Bachelor Home Companion* (1987).

'I've dreamed of cheese'

Somebody staring into the sky with the same ethereal appetite declared that the moon was made of green cheese. I never could conscientiously accept the full doctrine. I am a modernist in this matter. That the moon is made of cheese I have believed from childhood; and in the course of every month a giant (of my acquaintance) bites a big round piece out of it. This seems to me a doctrine that is above reason, but not contrary to it. But that the cheese is green seems to be in some degree actually contradicted by the senses and the reason; first because if the moon were made of green cheese it would be inhabited; and second because if it were made of green cheese it would be green. A blue moon is said to be an unusual sight; but I cannot think that a green one is much more common. In fact, I think I have seen the moon looking like every other sort of cheese except a green cheese. I have seen it look exactly like a cream cheese: a circle of warm white upon a warm faint violet sky above a cornfield in Kent. I have seen it look very like a Dutch cheese, rising a dull red copper disk amid masts and dark waters at Honfleur. I have seen it look like an ordinary sensible Cheddar cheese in an ordinary sensible Prussian blue sky; and I have once seen it so naked and ruinous-looking, so strangely lit up, that it looked like a Gruyère cheese, that awful volcanic cheese that has horrible holes in it, as if it had come in boiling unnatural milk from mysterious and unearthly cattle. But I have never yet seen the lunar cheese green: and I incline to the opinion that the moon is not old enough.

G. K. Chesterton, 'The Appetite of earth' (1939).

'Marooned three years agone,' he continued, 'and lived on goats since then, and berries, and oysters. Wherever a man is, says I, a man can do for himself. But, mate, my heart is sore for Christian diet. You mightn't happen to have a piece of cheese about you, now? No? Well, many's the long night I've dreamed of cheese – toasted, mostly – and woke up again, and here I were.'

'If ever I can get aboard again,' said I, 'you shall have cheese by the stone.'

Robert Louis Stevenson, *Treasure Island* (1883).

Mr Palomar is standing in line in a cheese shop, in Paris. He wants to buy certain goat cheeses that are preserved in oil in little transparent containers and spiced with various herbs and condiments. The line of customers moves along a counter where samples of the most unusual and disparate specialities are displayed. This is a shop whose range seems meant to document every conceivable form of dairy product; the very sign *'Spécialités froumagères'*, with that rare archaic or vernacular adjective, advises that here is guarded the legacy of a knowledge accumulated by a civilization through all its history and geography.

Three or four girls in pink smocks wait on the customers. The moment one of the girls is free she deals with the first in line and asks him to express his wishes; the customer names or, more often, points moving about the shop towards the object of his specific and expert appetites.

At that moment the whole line moves forward one place; and the person who till then had been standing beside the 'Bleu d'Auvergne' veined with green now finds himself at the level of the 'Brin d'amour', whose whiteness holds strands of dried straw stuck to it; the customer contemplating a ball wrapped in leaves can now concentrate on a cube dusted with ash. At each move forward, some customers are inspired by new stimuli and new desires: they may change their minds about what they were about to ask for or may add a new item to the list; and there are also those who never allow themselves to be distracted even for a moment from the objective they are pursuing – every different, fortuitous suggestion serves only to limit, through exclusion, the field of what they stubbornly want.

Palomar's spirit vacillates between contrasting urges: the one that aims at complete, exhaustive knowledge and could be satisfied only by tasting all the varieties; and the one that tends towards an absolute choice, the identification of the cheese that is his alone, a cheese that certainly exists even if he cannot recognize it (cannot recognize himself in it).

Or else, or else: it is not a matter of choosing the right cheese, but of being chosen. There is a reciprocal relationship between cheese and customer: each cheese awaits its customer, poses so as to attract him, with a firmness or a somewhat haughty graininess, or on the contrary, by melting in submissive abandon.

There is a hint of complicity hovering in the air: the refinement of the taste buds, and especially of the olfactory organs, has its moments of weakness, of loss of class, when the cheeses on their platters seem to proffer themselves as if on the divans of a brothel. A perverse grin flickers in the satisfaction of debasing the object of one's own gluttony with lowering nicknames: *crottin, boule de moine, bouton de culotte.*

This is not the kind of acquaintance that Mr Palomar is most inclined to pursue: he would be content to establish the simplicity of a direct physical relationship between man and cheese. But as in place of the cheeses he sees names of cheeses, concepts of cheeses, meanings of cheeses, histories of cheeses, contexts of cheeses, psychologies of cheeses, when he does not so much know as sense that behind each of theses cheeses there is all that, then his relationship becomes very complicated.

The cheese shop appears to Palomar the way an encyclopedia looks to an autodidact; he could memorize all the names, venture classification according to the forms – cake of soap, cylinder, done, ball – according to the consistency – dry, buttery, creamy, veined, firm – according to the alien materials involved in the crust or in the heart – raisins, pepper, walnuts, sesame seeds, herbs, molds – but this would not bring him a step closer to true knowledge, which lies in the experience of the flavors, composed of memory and imagination at once. Only on the basis of that could he establish a scale of preferences and tastes and curiosities and exclusions.

Behind every cheese there is a pasture of a different green under a different sky: meadow caked with salt that the tides of Normandy deposit every evening; meadows scented with aromas in the windy sunlight of Provence; there are different flocks with their stablings and their transhumances; there are secret processes handed down over the centuries. This shop is a museum: Mr Palomar, visiting it, feels, as he does in the Louvre, behind every displayed object the presence of the civilization that has given it form and takes form from it.

This shop is a dictionary; the language is the system of cheeses as a whole: a language whose morphology records declensions and conjugations in countless variants, and whose lexicon presents an inexhaustible richness of synonyms, idiomatic usages, connotations and nuances of meaning, as in all languages nourished by the contribution of a hundred dialects. It is a language made up of things; its nomenclature is only an external aspect, instrumental; but, for Mr Palomar, learning a bit of nomenclature remains still the first measure to be taken if he wants to stop for a moment the things that are flowing before his eyes.

From his pocket he takes a notebook, a pen, begins to write down some names, marking beside each name some feature that will enable him to recall the image to his memory; he tries also to make a synthetic sketch of the shape. He writes 'Pavé d'Airvault' and notes 'green mould', draws a flat parallelopiped and to one side notes '4cm. circa'; he writes 'St-Maure', notes 'gray granular cylinder with a little shaft inside' and draws it, measuring it at a glance as about '20cm'; then he writes 'Chabicholi' and draws another little cylinder.

'*Monsieur! Hoo there! Monsieur!*' A young cheese-girl, dressed in pink, is standing in front of him, as he is occupied with his notebook. It is his turn, he is next; in the line behind him everyone is observing his incongruous behaviour, heads are being shaken with those half-ironic, half-exasperated looks with which the inhabitants of the big cities consider the ever-increasing number of the mentally retarded wandering about the streets.

The elaborate and greedy order that he intended to make momentarily slips his mind; he stammers; he falls back on the most obvious, the most banal, the most advertised, as if the automatons of mass civilization were waiting only for this moment of uncertainty on his part in order to seize him again and have him at their mercy.

Italo Calvino, *Mr Palomar* (1985).

I remember a friend of mine buying a couple of cheeses at Liverpool. Splendid cheeses they were, ripe and mellow, and with a two hundred horse-power scent about them that might have been warranted to carry three miles, and knock a man over at two hundred yards. I was in Liverpool at the time, and my friend said that if I didn't mind he would get me to take them back with me to London, as he did not think the cheeses ought to be kept much longer. 'Oh with pleasure, dear boy,' I replied, 'with pleasure.' I called for the cheeses, and took them away in a cab. It was a ramshackle affair, dragged along by a knock-kneed broken-winded somnambulist, which his owner in a moment of enthusiasm, during conversation, referred to as a horse. I put the cheeses on the top, and we started off at a shamble that would have done credit to the swiftest steam-roller ever built, and all went merry as a funeral bell, until we turned a corner. There, the wind carried a whiff from the cheeses full on our steed. It woke him up, and with a sort of terror, he dashed off at three miles an hour. The wind still blew in his direction, and before we reached the end of the street he was laying himself out at the rate of nearly four miles an hour, leaving the cripples and the old ladies simply nowhere. It took two porters as well as the driver to hold him in at the station; and I do not think they would have done it, even then, had not one of the men had the presence of mind to put a handkerchief over his nose, and to light a bit of brown paper. I took my ticket, and marched proudly up the platform, with my cheese, the people falling back respectfully on either side. The train was crowded, and I had to get into a carriage where there were already seven other people. One crusty old gentleman objected, but I got in, notwithstanding; and, putting my cheeses upon the rack, squeezed down with a pleasant smile, and said it was a warm day. A few moments passed, and then the old gentleman began to fidget. 'Very close in here,' he said. 'Quite oppressive,' said the man next to him. And then they both began sniffing, and, at the third sniff, they caught it right on the chest, and rose up without another word and went out. And then a stout lady got up, and said it was disgraceful that a respectable married woman should be harried about in this way, and gathered up a bag and eight parcels and went. The remaining four passengers sat on for a while, until a solemn-looking man in the corner who, from his dress and general appearance, seemed to belong to the undertaker class, said it put him in mind of a dead baby; and the other three passengers tried to get out of the door at the same time, and hurt themselves.

Jerome K. Jerome, *Three Men in a Boat* (1889).

After a few sentences exchanged at long intervals in the manner of rustic courtesy, I inquired casually what was the name of the town. The old lady answered that its name was Stilton, and composedly continued her needlework. But I had paused with my mug in the air, and was gazing at her with a suddenly arrested concern. 'I suppose,' I said, 'that it has nothing to do with the cheese of that name?'

'Oh yes,' she answered, with a staggering indifference, 'they used to make it here.'

I put down my mug with a gravity far greater than her own. 'But this place is a shrine!' I said. 'Pilgrims should be pouring into it from wherever the English legend has endured alive. There ought to be a colossal statue in the market-place of the man who invented Stilton cheese. There ought to be another colossal statue of the first cow who provided the foundations of it. There should be a burnished tablet let into the ground of the spot where some courageous man first ate Stilton cheese, and survived. On the top of a neighbouring hill (if there are any neighbouring hills) there should be a huge model of a Stilton cheese, made of some rich green marble and engraven with some haughty motto: I suggested something like '*Ver non simper viret; sed Stiltonia simper virescit.*' The old lady said 'yes, sir,' and continued her domestic occupations.

G.K. Chesterton, 'The Poet and the Cheese' (1934).

'Exquisite preparations of eggs'

'How quick your servants are!' Miss Quested exclaimed. For a cloth had already been laid, with a vase of artificial flowers in its centre, and Mahmoud Ali's butler offered them poached eggs and tea for the second time.

'I thought we would eat this before our caves, and breakfast after.'

'Isn't this breakfast?'

'This breakfast? Did you think I should treat you so strangely?' He had been warned that English people never stop eating, and that he had better nourish them every two hours until a solid meal was ready.

E.M. Forster, *A Passage to India* (1924).

'We are two resolute women – I mean that *she* is resolute, and that I follow here – and we have asserted our right of dining to our own satisfaction, by means of an interview with the chief cook. This interesting person is an ex-Zouave in the French army. Instead of making excuses, he confessed that the barbarous tastes of the English and American visitors had so discouraged him, that he had lost all pride and pleasure in the exercise of his art. As an example of what he meant, he mentioned his experience of two young Englishmen who could speak no foreign language. The waiters reported that they objected to their breakfasts, and especially to the eggs. Thereupon (to translate the Frenchman's way of putting it) he exhausted himself in exquisite preparations of eggs. *Eggs à la tripe, au gratin, à l'Aurore, à la Dauphine, à la Poulette, à la Tartare, à la Venitienne, à la Bordelaise*, and so on, and so on. Still the two young gentlemen were not satisfied. The ex-Zouave, infuriated, wounded in his honour, disgraced as a professor, insisted on an explanation. What, in heaven's name, *did* they want for breakfast? They wanted boiled eggs; and a fish which they called a *Bloaterre*. It was impossible, he said, to express his contempt for the English idea of a breakfast, in the presence of ladies. You know how a cat expresses herself in the presence of a dog – and you will understand the allusion.

Wilkie Collins, *I Say No* (1884).

Harris proposed that we should have scrambled eggs for breakfast. He said he would cook them. It seemed, from his account, that he was very good at doing scrambled eggs. He often did them at picnics and when out on yachts. He was quite famous for them. People who had once tasted his scrambled eggs, so we gathered from his conversation, never cared for any other food afterwards, but pined away and died when they could not get them.

Jerome K. Jerome, *Three Men in a Boat* (1889).

I had an excellent repast – the best repast possible – which consisted simply of boiled eggs and bread and butter. It was the quality of these simple ingredients that made the occasion memorable. The eggs were so good that I am ashamed to say how many of them I consumed . . . it might seem that an egg which has succeeded in being fresh has done all that can reasonably be expected of it.

Henry James, *A Little Tour of France* (1884).

I realized that I was eating something quite out of the ordinary – soft boiled eggs wrapped in a covering of meat-jelly flavoured with herbs and slightly iced.

To please Marambot, I smacked my lips and said: 'This *is* good!'

He smiled. 'Two things are needed for it – good jelly, which isn't easy to come by, and good eggs. How rare good eggs are! The yolk ought to be slightly red and really tasty. I keep two hen-runs, one for eggs and one for the table. I feed my laying hens in a special way, on a theory of my own. In an egg, as in the flesh of a chicken, or in beef or mutton or milk – in everything in fact – there persists, and one ought to be able to taste, the flavour, the quintessence of the animal's previous feeding. How much better food would be if people took more trouble about that!'

Guy de Maupassant, 'Madame Husson's May King' (1888).

'Pan de Dios'

She learned to make Bread partly from recollecting how she had *seen* an old servant set to work and she used to say that the *first* time she attempted Brown bread, it was with *awe*. She mixed the dough and saw it rise – and then she put it into the oven and sat down to watch the oven door with feelings like Benvuti Cellini when he watched his Perseus put into the

Furnace. She did not feel too sure what it would come out! But it came out a beautiful crusty loaf very light and sweet, and proud of it she was.

Thomas Carlyle, *Reminiscences* (1881).

There are some curious customs about bread which were strictly observed in my village, and indeed through the whole of Andalusia. Before cutting a new loaf it was proper to make the sign of the cross over it with a knife. If a *olaf* or *rosca* fell to the ground, the person who picked it up would kiss it and say '*Es pan de Dios*' ('It's God's bread'). Children were never allowed to strike it or treat it roughly or to crumble it on the table, and it was considered shocking to offer even stale crusts to a dog.

Gerald Brenan, *South from Granada* (1957).

English working people everywhere, so far as I know, refuse brown bread; it is usually impossible to buy wholemeal bread in a working-class district. They sometimes give the reason that brown bread is 'dirty'. I suspect the real reason is that in the past brown bread has been confused with black bread, which is traditionally associated with Popery and wooden shoes.

George Orwell, *The Road to Wigan Pier* (1937).

My sister had a trenchant way of cutting our bread-and-butter for us, that never varied. First, with her left hand she jammed the loaf hard and fast against her bib – where it sometimes got a pin into it, and sometimes a needle, which we afterwards got into our mouths. Then she took some butter (not too much) on a knife and spread it on the loaf, in an apothecary kind of way, as if she were making a plaister – using both sides of the knife with a slapping dexterity, and trimming and moulding the butter off round the crust. Then, she gave the knife a final smart wipe on the edge of the plaister, and then sawed a very thick round off the loaf: which she finally, before separating from the loaf, hewed into two halves, of which Joe got one, and I the other.

Charles Dickens, *Great Expectations* (1861).

Ron's wreck of a mother used to give us buttered bread with hundreds and thousands on it. It was like being handed a slice of powdered rainbow.

Clive James, *Unreliable Memoirs* (1980).

To set but a low value upon toast is to expose one's deficiencies in right appreciation.

'To make toast properly,' says the admirable Mrs. Beeton, 'a great deal of attention is required; much more, indeed, than people generally suppose. Never use new bread for making any kind of taste, as it renders it heavy, and besides, is very extravagant.' A loaf one day old is the best material. Mrs Beeton continues: 'Dry toast should be more gradually made than buttered toast, as its great beauty consists in its crispness, and this cannot be attained unless the process is slow, and the bread is allowed gradually to colour.' Dry toast, one might add, should be thin as well as crisp. It should be eaten within, at the most, ten minutes of leaving the fire. While awaiting its turn on the table, each piece of toast should stand alone, on no account being laid flat or placed so close to another piece that it touches. Stale toast, or toast from which the crispness has, as it were, thawed away, is abomination. It is limp, and tough, and indigent. Moreover, the mastication of it makes no sound. Now the noise from good toast should reverberate in the head like the thunder of July.

E.V. Lucas, 'When Toasters Disagree' (1906).

On 10th March, Haydon spent an evening with Mrs. Siddons to hear her read *Macbeth*. 'She acts Macbeth herself,' he writes, 'better than either Kemble or Kean.' It is extraordinary the awe this wonderful woman inspires. After her first reading the men retired to tea. While we were all eating toast and tinkling cups and saucers, she began again. It was like the effect of a mass bell at Madrid. All noise ceased; we slunk to our seats like boors, two or three of the most distinguished men of the day, with the very toast in their mouths, afraid to bite. It was curious to see Lawrence in this predicament, to hear him bite by degrees, and then stop for fear of making too much crackle, his eyes full of water from the constraint; and at the same time to hear Mrs Siddons' 'eye of newt and toe of frog!' and then to see Lawrence give a sly bite, and then look awed and pretend to be listening. I went away highly gratified.

A. Penrose, *The Autobiography and Memoirs of Benjamin Robert Haydon* (1927).

There was good dripping toast by the fire in the evening. Good jelly dripping and crusty, home-baked bread, with the mealy savour of ripe wheat roundly in your mouth and under your teeth, roasted sweet and crisp and deep brown, and covered with little pockets where the dripping will hide and melt and shine in the light, deep down inside, ready to run when your teeth bite in.

Richard Llewellyn, *How Green was my Valley* (1939).

When the girl returned, some hours later, she carried a tray, with a cup of fragrant tea steaming on it; and a plate piled up with very hot buttered toast, cut thick, very brown on both sides, with the butter running through the holes in it in great golden drops, like honey from the honey-comb. The smell of that buttered toast simply talked to Toad, and with no uncertain voice; talked of warm kitchens, of breakfasts on bright frosty mornings, of cosy parlour firesides on winter evenings, when one's ramble was over and slippered feet were propped on the fender; of the purring of contented cats, and the twitter of sleepy canaries. Toad sat up on end once more, dried his eyes, sipped his tea and munched his toast.

Kenneth Graham, *The Wind in the Willows* (1908).

'A steady contemplative browsing': salad

So I think I have answered all thy questions except about Morgan's cos lettuce. The first personal peculiarity I ever observed of him (all worthy souls are subject to 'em) was a particular kind of rabbit like delight in munching salads with oil without vinegar – after dinner – a steady contemplative browsing on them.

Charles Lamb, letter to Samuel Taylor Coleridge, 26 August, 1814.

Salad, I can't bear salad. It grows while you're eating it, you know. Have you noticed? You start one side of your plate and by the time you've got to the other, there's a fresh crop of lettuce taken root and sprouted up.

Alan Ayckbourn, *Living Together* (1975).

Ther ought t' be some way t' eat celery so it wouldn' sound like you wuz steppin' on a basket.

Kin Hubbard, *Abe Martin's Wisecracks* (1930).

It has been a common saying of physicians in England, that a cucumber should be well sliced, and dressed with pepper and vinegar, and then thrown out, as good for nothing.

Samuel Johnson, quoted by James Boswell, *The Journal of a Tour to the Hebrides with Samuel Johnson* (1786).

One thing, however, is truly delicious in Spain – the salad, to compound which, says the Spanish proverb, four persons are wanted: a spendthrift for oil, a miser for vinegar, a counsellor for salt, and a madman to stir it all up. N.B. – Get the biggest bowl you can, in order that this latter operation may be thoroughly performed. The salad is the glory of every French dinner, and the disgrace of most in England, even in good houses, and from two simple causes; first, from the putting in eggs, mustard, and other heretical ingredients, and, secondly, from making it long before it is wanted to be eaten, whereby the green materials, which should be crisp and fresh, become sodden and leathery.

Richard Ford, *Gatherings from Spain* (1846).

'The salad is the glory of the French dinner and the disgrace of most in England'; this remark of a British traveller, Captain Ford, in 1846 holds true as ever it did, in the assemblages that were created at my brother's aforementioned school St Botolph's, for example, – a few melancholy slices of cucumber, an approximately washed lettuce (iceberg, naturally), which appeared to have been shredded by wild dogs, two entire radish heads (served whole, presumably to avoid the risk of their proving edible in sliced form), a pale and watery quarter of tomato, the whole ensemble accompanied by a salad cream that at least had the virtue of tasting 'like itself' – that's to say, like the by-product of an industrial accident.

John Lanchester, *The Debt to Pleasure* (1996).

'Delight in butchered food'

Your butcher breathes an atmosphere of good living. The beef mingles kindly with his animal nature. He grows fat with the best of it. Perhaps with inhaling its very essence; and has no time to grow spare, theoretical and hypochondriacal.

Leigh Hunt, *The Seer; Or, Common Places Refreshed* (1841).

Besides the *corn market* at Warminster, I was delighted, and greatly surprised, to see the *meat*. Not only the very finest *veal* and *lamb* that I had ever seen in my life, but so exceedingly beautiful, that I could hardly believe my eyes. I am a great connoisseur in joints of meat; a great judge, if five-and-thirty years of experience can give sound judgment. I verily believe that I have bought and have roasted more whole sirloins of beef than any man in England.

William Cobbett, *Rural Rides* (1830).

We had for dinner a Calf's Head, boiled Fowl and Tongue, a Saddle of Mutton roasted on the Side Table, and a fine Swan roasted with Currant Jelly sauce for the first Course. The second Course a couple of Wild Fowl called Dun Fowls, Larks, Blamange, tarts etc. etc. and a good Desert of Fruit after amongst which was a damson cheese. I never eat a bit of a Swan before, and I think it good eating with sweet sauce. The Swan was killed 3 weeks before it was eat and yet not the least bad taste in it.

James Woodforde, diary entry, 28 January, 1780.

After the carcass had been singed, the pig-sticker would pull off the detachable, grizzly, outer covering of the toes, known locally as 'the shoes', and fling them among the children, who scrambled for, then sucked and gnawed them, straight from the filth of the sty and blackened by fire as they were.

Flora Thompson, *Lark Rise to Candleford* (1939).

She filled a small crockery bowl and set it on the table. 'Sit down,' she said. 'Eat. When you've tried it, I'll tell you the secret ingredient.'

Steam rose from the bowl, with a smell so deep and spicy that already he felt overfed. He accepted the spoon that she held out. He dipped it in the spoon reluctantly and took a sip.

'Well?' she asked.

'It's very good,' he said.

In fact, it was delicious, if you cared about such things. He'd never tasted soup so good. There were chunks of fresh vegetables, and the broth was rich and heavy. He took another mouthful. Ruth stood over him, her thumbs hooked into her blue jeans pockets. 'Chicken feet,' she said.

'Pardon?'

'Chicken feet is the secret ingredient.'

He lowered his spoon and looked down into the bowl.

'Eat up,' she told him. 'Put some meat on your bones.'

Anne Tyler, *Dinner at the Homesick Restaurant* (1982).

A large dairy animal approached Zaphod Beeblebrox's table, a large fat meaty quadruped of the bovine type with large water eyes, small horns and what might almost have been an ingratiating smile on its lips.

'Good evening,' it lowed and sat back heavily on its haunches, 'I am the main Dish of the Day. May I interest you in parts of my body?' It harrumphed and gurgled a bit, wriggled its hindquarters into a more comfortable position and gazed peacefully at them.

Its gaze was met by looks of startled bewilderment from Arthur and Trillian, a resigned shrug from Ford Prefect and naked hunger from Zaphod Beeblebrox.

'Something off the shoulder perhaps?' suggested the animal. 'Braised in a white wine sauce?'

'Er, *your* shoulder?' said Arthur in a horrified whisper.

'But naturally my shoulder, sir,' mooed the animal contentedly, 'nobody else's is mine to offer.'

Zaphod leapt to his feet and started prodding and feeling

the animal's shoulder appreciatively.

'Or the rump is very good,' murmured the animal. 'I've been exercising it and eating plenty of grain, so there's a lot of good meat there.' It gave a mellow grunt, gurgled again and started to chew the cud. It swallowed the cud again. 'Or a casserole of me perhaps?' it added.

'You mean this animal actually wants us to eat it?' whispered Trillian to Ford.

'Me?' said Ford, with a glazed look in his eyes, 'I don't mean anything.'

'That's absolutely horrible,' exclaimed Arthur, 'the most revolting thing I've ever heard.'

'What's the problem, Earthman?' said Zaphod, now transferring his attention to the animal's enormous rump.

'I just don't want to eat an animal that's standing there inviting me to,' said Arthur. 'It's heartless.'

'Better than eating an animal that doesn't want to be eaten,' said Zaphod.

'That's not the point,' Arthur protested. Then he thought about it for a moment. 'All right,' he said, 'maybe it is the point. I don't care, I'm not going to think about it now. I'll just . . . er . . .'

The Universe raged about him in its death throes.

'I think I'll just have a green salad,' he muttered.

Douglas Adams, The Hitchhiker's Guide to the Galaxy:
A Trilogy in Four Parts (1986).

I dined at the Chaplain's table upon a roasted Tongue and Udder. N.B. I shall not dine on a roasted Tongue and Udder again very soon.

James Woodforde, diary entry, 17 February, 1793.

I have been assured by a very knowing American of my acquaintance in London, That a young healthy child well nursed is at a year old a most delicious, nourishing, and whole-some food, whether stewed, roasted, baked, or boiled; and I make no doubt that it will equally serve in a fricassee or a ragout.

Jonathan Swift, A Modest Proposal (1729).

O my fellow men – do not defile your bodies with sinful foods. We have corn, we have apples, bending down the branches with their weight, and grapes swelling on the vines. There are sweet flavoured herbs, and vegetables which can be cooked and softened over the fire, nor are you denied milk, or thyme-scented honey. The earth affords a lavish supply of riches, of innocent foods, and offers you banquets that involve no bloodshed or slaughter; only beasts satisfy their hunger with flesh, and not even all of those, for horses, cattle, and sheep live on grass. But creatures whose nature is wild and fierce, Armenian tigers and raging lions, bears and wolves delight in butchered food. Alas, what wickedness to swallow flesh into our own flesh, to fatten our greedy bodies by cramming in other bodies, to have one living creature fed by the death of another! In the midst of such wealth as earth, the best of mothers, provides, nothing forsooth satisfies you, but to behave like the Cyclopes, inflicting sorry wounds with cruel teeth! You cannot appease the hungry cravings of your wicked gluttonous stomach, except by destroying some other life!

Ovid, Metamorphoses (AD 8).

'The touchstone is fish'

The Divine took his seat at the breakfast-table, and began to compose his spirits by the gentle sedative of a large cup of tea, the demulcent of a well-buttered muffin, and the tonic of a small lobster.

The Rev. Dr Folliott: You are a man of taste, Mr Crotchet. A man of taste is seen at once in the array of his breakfast-table. Chocolate, coffee, tea, cream, eggs, ham, tongue, cold fowl, – all these are good, and bespeak good knowledge in him who sets them forth: but the touchstone is fish; anchovy is the first step, prawns and shrimp the second; and I laud him who reaches even to these: potted chard and lampreys are the third, and a fine stretch of progression; but lobster is, indeed, matter for a May morning, and demands a rare combination of knowledge and virtue in him who sets it forth.

Thomas Love Peacock, *Crotchet Castle* (1823).

With regard to a John Dory, which you desire to be particularly informed about, . . . it hath not the moist, mellow, oleaginous, gliding, smooth descent from the tongue to the palate, thence the stomach, etc., as your Brighton turbot hath, which I take to be the most friendly and familiar flavour of any that swims – most genial and at home to the palate.

Nor has it, on the other hand, that fine falling-oft flakiness, that obsequious peeling off (as it were like a sea onion) which endears your cod's-head and shoulders to some appetites, that manly firmness, combined with a sort of womanish coming-in-pieces, which the same cod's-head and shoulders hath – where the *whole* is easily separable, pliant to a knife or spoon, but each *individual flake* presents a pleasing resistance to the opposed tooth – you understand me; these delicate subjects are necessarily obscure.

But it has a third flavour of its own, totally distinct from cod or turbot, which must be owned may to some not injudicious palates render it acceptable; but to my unpractised tooth it presented rather a crude river-fish-flavour, like your pike or carp, and perhaps, like them, should have been tamed and corrected by some laborious and well-chosen sauce. Still I always suspect a fish which requires so much of artificial settings-off. Your choicest relishes (like native loveliness) need not the foreign aid of ornament, but are, when unadorned (that is, with nothing but a little plain anchovy and a squeeze of lemon) – are then adorned the most.

Charles Lamb, letter to Charles Chambers, 1 September, 1817.

I was shown several varieties of fish here that were quiet useless for the home market because the English, even the poorest, will not touch them. They are re-shipped to the Continent, where folk are either wiser of less fastidious. One of these rejected fish was that horny pink fellow known to the trade as 'the swaddy', which is, of course, old-fashioned slang for 'soldier'. I heard a story of one trawler skipper hailing another in the Northern Seas and asking from where he had come. 'From Aldershot,' was the reply, in deepest disgust. 'I've got nothing so far but a load of so-and-so swaddies'. Kits of these fish had been sold that morning at three shillings each, and there would be easily enough in each kit to feed a large family for a week. I am not suggesting that any family should try to feed itself for a week on this fish; but there is nothing wrong with it – the French, whose palate is at least as good as ours, make great use of it, and I fancy I have eaten it myself in France – and it seems strange that this and a few other perfectly edible fish should still be totally rejected in a country where so many people are living miserably on bread and margarine. All the time I was being shown the huge Ice Factory and the Fish Meal and Oil Factories, I was wondering whether it would not be possible for an enterprising Ministry of Health to tackle this problem of diet, not in order to bully a lot of poor folk into eating things they do not want to eat, but in order to give the more enterprising housewives among them an opportunity of getting clear of the wretched tea and bread and margarine and fried potato fare without spending any more money. It seems ridiculous that, every day, tons and tons of quiet edible and wholesome fish should be brought here and then exported at a cheap rate, simply because there is against such fish a popular prejudice, dating probably from the good old give-me-a-thick-beefsteak days, when we were all hard at work and could live like lords.

J.B. Priestley, *English Journey* (1934).

I attended to my trout with a kind of surgical distaste. Its slightly open barbed mouth and its tiny round eye, which had half erupted while grilling, like the core of a pustule, were unusually recriminatory. I sliced the head off and put it on my side-plate and then proceeded to remove the pale flesh from the bones with the flat of my knife. It was quite flavourless, except that, where its innards had been imperfectly removed, silvery traces of roe gave it an unpleasant bitterness.

Alan Hollinghurst, *The Swimming-pool Library* (1988).

'I think oysters are more beautiful than any religion,' he resumed presently. 'They not only forgive our unkindness to them; they justify it, they incite us to go on being perfectly horrid to them. Once they arrive at the supper-table they seem to enter thoroughly into the spirit of the thing. There's nothing in Christianity or Buddhism that quite matches the sympathetic unselfishness of an oyster.

H.H. Munro (Saki), 'The Match-maker' (1911).

He was a bold man that first ate an oyster.

Jonathan Swift, *Polite Conversation* (1738).

K. wants to make a seafood salad, so we go into a fishmonger's on Bleecker. A young, fat guy sits by the door, an old, grey one at the back, and, doing all the work, a Puerto Rican.

K.: I want a dozen mussels.

FAT GUY: We don't sell them by the dozen.

K.: How do you sell them?

FAT GUY: Sell them by the pound.

K.: OK. A pound. (pause) How many are there in a pound?

FAT GUY: (triumphantly) 'Bout a dozen.

Alan Bennett, Writing Home (1990).

And there is good fresh trout for supper. My mother used to put them on a hot stone over the fire, wrapped in breadcrumbs, butter, parsley and lemon rind, all bound about with the fresh green leaves of leeks. If there is better food in heaven, I am in a hurry to be there, if not I will not be thought wicked for saying so.

Richard Llewellyn, How Green Was My Valley (1939).

I am wondering where Evelyn got the sushi – the tuna, yellowtail, mackerel, shrimp, eel, even bonito, all seem so fresh and there are piles of wasabi and clumps of ginger placed strategically around the Wilton platter – but I also like the idea that I *don't* know, will *never* know, will never *ask* where it came from and that the sushi will sit there in the middle of the glass table from Zona that Evelyn's father bought her like some mysterious apparition from the Orient.

Bret Easton Ellis, American Psycho (1991).

They sat in the cold mess-hall, most of them eating with their hats on, eating slowly, picking out putrid little fish from under the leaves of boiled black cabbage and spitting the bones out under the table. When the bones formed a heap and it was the turn of another team, someone would sweep them off and they'd be trodden into a mush on the floor. But it was considered bad manners to spit the fish-bones straight out on the floor.

Alexander Solzhenitsyn, One Day in the Life of Ivan Denisovich (1962).

'Sweet cake her daily bread'

At all ordinary diet and plain beverage she would pout; but she fed on creams and ices like a humming-bird on honey-paste. Sweet wine was her element, and sweet cake her daily bread.

Charlotte Brontë, *Villette* (1853).

Rosa went off to Fubsby's, that magnificent shop at the corner of Parliament Place and Alicompayne Square, – a shop into which the rogue had often cast a glance of approbation as he passed: for there are not only the most wonderful and delicious cakes and confections in the window, but at the counter there are almost sure to be three or four of the prettiest women in the whole of this world, with little darling caps of the last French make, with beautiful wavy hair, and the neatest possible waists and aprons.

Yes, there they sit; and others, perhaps, besides Fitz have cast a sheep's-eye through those enormous plate-glass windowpanes. I suppose it is the fact of perpetually living among such a quality of good things that makes those young ladies so beautiful. They come into the place, let us say, like ordinary people, and gradually grow handsomer and handsomer, until they grow out into the perfect angels you see. It can't be otherwise: if you and I, my dear fellow, were to have a course of that place, we should become beautiful too. They live in an atmosphere of the most delicious pine-apples, blanc-manges, creams (some whipt, and some so good that of course they don't want whipping), jellies, tipsy-cakes, cherry-brandy – one hundred sweet and lovely things. Look at the preserved fruits, look at the golden ginger, the outspread ananas, the darling little rogues of China oranges, ranged in the gleaming crystal cylinders. Mon Dieu! Look at the strawberries in the leaves. Each of them is as large nearly as a lady's reticule, and looks as if it had been brought up in a nursery to itself. One of those strawberries is a meal for these young ladies, behind the counter; they nibble off a little from the side, and if they are very hungry, which can scarcely every happen, they are allowed to go to the crystal canisters and take out a rout-cake or macaroon.

William Makepeace Thackeray, 'A Little Dinner at Timmin's' (1848).

Then four times during the two hours' period of her conversazione tea and cake were to be handed round on salvers. It is astonishing how far a very little cake will go in this way, particularly if administered tolerably early after dinner. The men can't eat it, and the women, having no plates and no table, are obliged to abstain. Mrs Jones knows that she cannot hold a piece of crumbly cake in her hand till it be consumed without doing serious injury to her best dress.

Anthony Trollope, *Framley Parsonage* (1861).

The knife descended on the puff and it was in two, but the result was not satisfactory to Tom, for he still eyed the halves doubtfully. At last he said –

'Shut your eyes, Maggie.'

'What for?'

'You never mind what for. Shut 'em, when I tell you.'

Maggie obeyed.

'Now, which'll you have, Maggie – right hand or left?'

'I'll have that with the jam run out,' said Maggie, keeping her eyes shut to please Tom.

'Why, you don't like that, you silly. You may have it if it comes to you fair, but I shan't give it you without. Right or left – you choose, now. Ha-a-a!' said Tom, in a tone of exasperation, as Maggie peeped. 'You keep your eyes shut now, else you shan't have any.'

Maggie's power of sacrifice did not extend so far; indeed, I fear she cared less that Tom should enjoy the utmost possible amount of puff, than that he should be pleased with her for giving him the best bit. So she shut her eyes quite close, till Tom told her to 'say which', and then she said, 'Left hand.'

'You've got it,' said Tom, in rather a bitter tone.

'What! the bit with the jam run out?'

'No; here, take it,' said Tom, firmly, handing decidedly the best piece to Maggie.

'Oh, please, Tom, have it: I don't mind – I like the other: please take this.'

'No, I shan't,' said Tom, almost crossly, beginning on his own inferior piece.

George Eliot, *The Mill on the Floss* (1860).

Very different from our own brother who used to spend his weekly pocket money, one penny, on an ounce of the best chocolate milk and cram it all into his mouth at once, saying he liked *one good taste*. My sister and I preferred quantity to quality and felt it rather hard that he should then expect us to share our sweets with him when he had nothing to offer in exchange. Golden pralines with a mushy centre were a favourite, but fruit-drops went further and humbugs, striped like zebras, lasted longest of all and were so hot that one had to move them hastily from one cheek to the other. Then there were little bags of sherbet, four a penny, with a hollow black liquorice stick through which one drew it up till it fizzed in one's mouth and tickled the throat pleasantly. Once I purchased some tiny silver balls which were fashionable then for decorating wedding cakes, but they were a great disappointment, the silver sucked off at once and the minute ball, highly scented with peppermint, was difficult to anchor.

Audrey Earle, 'Nursery memories' (1972).

Most of those not eating are sucking – mintoes, caramels, pear drops, acid drops, mint imperials, Pontefract cakes (pastilles of embossed liquorice), fish-shaped sweets or jelly babies. 'Nice spice,' they murmur to one another as they walk, almost lisping in suck. And some of them as they bite into a succulent portion, slow and halt as if to concentrate, frozen in the chomp.

Paul West, 'Voices of England's Past' (1984).

The Fine Arts are five in number: Painting, Music, Poetry, Sculpture, and Architecture – wherof the principal branch is Confectionary.

Marie Antoine Carême, quoted by Anatole France in *The Crime of Sylvestre Bonnard* (1881).

The great charm of treacle is in its transit from the pot to the plate; in no other liquid, except the exquisite thin honey of Switzerland, is it possible to trace one's autograph. Most of us as children saw our names writ in treacle.

E.V. Lucas, 'Concerning Breakfast', from *Fireside and Sunshine* (1906).

My good old aunt, who never parted from me at the end of a holiday without stuffing a sweetmeat, or some nice thing into my pocket, had dismissed me one evening with a smoking plum-cake fresh from the oven. On my way to school (it was over London Bridge) a grey-headed old beggar saluted me (I have no doubt at this time of day that he was a counterfeit). I had no pence to console him with, and in the vanity of self-denial, and the very coxcombry of charity, school-boy-like, I made him a present of – the whole cake! I walked on a little, buoyed up, as one is on such occasions, with a sweet soothing of self-satisfaction; but before I had got to the end of the bridge, my better feelings returned, and I burst into tears, thinking how ungrateful I had been to my good aunt, to go and give her good gift away to a stranger, that I had never seen before, and who might be a bad man for aught I knew; and then I thought of the pleasure my aunt would be taking in thinking that I – I myself, and not another – would eat her nice cake – and what should I say to her the next time I saw her – how naughty I was to part with her pretty present – and the odour of that spicy cake came back upon my recollection, and the pleasure and the curiosity I had taken in seeing her make it, and her joy when she sent it to the oven, and how disappointed she would feel that I had never had a bit of it in my mouth at last – and I blamed the impertinent spirit of alms-giving, and out-of-place hypocrisy of goodness, and above all I wished never to see the face again of that insidious, good-for-nothing, old grey impostor.

Charles Lamb, 'A Dissertation upon Roast Pig' (1823).

The day Quick turned twelve his father baked him a cake and wrote his name in icing and stuck twelve candles in it, and when the evening rush at the shop was over, the Lamb family came through from the counter to the kitchen to sit around the oval table and sing 'Happy Birthday.' They'd just finished the singing and were into the three cheers when the cowbell rang up front and Oriel went to serve in the shop. She came back at a jog.

Lady wants a cake, Les. She's desperate. She'll give us a quid.

It's too much. We haven't got one.

Quick looked at the candles, still smoking.

It's too much, said Lester.

Quick watched as his mother whipped out all the candles, smoothed the icing over with a knife and gathered the cake up under her arm to charge back down the corridor.

Birthday, Quick, said Fish.

Yeah, said Quick.

Suddenly, they all laughed – even Quick. It started as a titter,

and went quickly to a giggle, then a wheeze, and then scream-
ing and shrieking till they were daft with it, and when Oriel
came back in they were pandemonius, gone for all money. But
they paused like good soldiers when she solemnly raised her
hand. She fished in her apron and pulled out a florin. Happy
birthday, son.

You want change from this? said Quick.

They set off again and there was no stopping them.

Tim Winton, *Cloudstreet* (1991).

Call me old school, but I think it should be compulsory for a
birthday cake to have jam, icing and candles. People who make
birthday cakes with wholegrain flour and decorate them with
sunflower seeds should be given a community service order
and be compelled to go to punitive cake-making classes.

Sue Townsend, *Adrian Mole and the Weapons of Mass Destruction*
(2004).

And suddenly the memory revealed itself. The taste was that
of the little piece of Madeleine which on Sunday mornings at
Combray, (because on those mornings I did not go out before
mass), when I went to say good morning to her in her bed-
room, my aunt Leonie used to give me, dipping it first in her
own cup of tea or tisane. The sight of the little Madeleine had
recalled nothing to my mind before I tasted it; perhaps because
I had so often seen such things in the meantime, without tasting them, on the trays in pastry-cooks' windows, that their
image had dissociated itself from those Combray days to take
its place among others more recent.

Marcel Proust, *The Remembrance of Things Past* (1913).

Shortbread has beneficial effects on the soul. The warm
glow it gives is better than alcohol, and more readily available
than sex. Only 90p for a box (cardboard) of the best brand.

Doesn't always work though.

Lucy Ellmann, *Sweet Desserts* (1988).

I had one of the coffees with whipped cream, and a big piece of carrot cake. I ate the cake eagerly, cramming it into my mouth as if it were a drug, somehow feeling this would give me strength for whatever was to happen with Ray. 'I like to watch you eat,' Ray said, looking at me dreamy-eyed. I wiped off my chin with a napkin; the cake had abruptly become quite tasteless.

Tama Janowitz, *Slaves of New York* (1986).

'Favoured beverage of the intellectual'

Tea, though ridiculed by those who are naturally coarse in their nervous sensibilities, or are become so from wine-drinking, and are not susceptible of influence from so refined a stimulant, will always be the favoured beverage of the intellectual.

Thomas de Quincey, *Confessions of an English Opium-Eater* (1821).

What a curious thing it was, that all of a sudden the remotest nation of the East, otherwise unknown, and foreign to all our habits, should convey to us a domestic custom which changed the face of our morning refreshments; and that, instead of ale and meat, or wine, all the polite part of England should be drinking a Chinese infusion, and setting up earthenware in their houses, painted with preposterous scenery!

Leigh Hunt, 'The Subject of Breakfast Continued: Tea-drinking' (1834)

Tea had come as a deliverer to a land that called for deliverance; a land of beef and ale, of heavy eating and abundant drunkenness; of grey skies and harsh winds; of strong-nerved, stout-purposed, slow-thinking men and women. Above all, a land of sheltered homes and warm firesides – firesides that were waiting – waiting, for the bubbling kettle and the fragrant breath of tea.

Agnes Repplier, *To Think of Tea!* (1932).

What a part of confidante has that poor teapot played ever since the kindly plant was introduced among us. Why myriads of women have cried over it, to be sure! What sickbeds it has smoked by! What fevered lips have received refreshment from it! Nature meant very kindly by women when she made the tea plant; and with a little thought, what a series of pictures and groups the fancy may conjure up and assemble round the teapot and cup.

William Makepiece Thackeray, *The History of Pendennis* (1850).

Thank God for tea! What would the world do without tea? How did it exist? I am glad I was not born before tea.

Sidney Smith, quoted by Hesketh Pearson in *The Smith of Smiths* (1934).

For here now, in the space of a few hours I was a dull and a miserable, a clever and a happy mortal, and all without the intervention of any external cause, except a dish of green tea, which indeed is a most kind remedy in cases of this kind. Often I have found relief from it. I am so fond of green tea I could write a whole dissertation on its virtues. It comforts and enlivens without the risks attendant on spirituous liquors. Gentle herb! Let the florid grape yield to thee. Thy soft influence is a more safe inspirer of social joy.

James Boswell, journal entry, 13 February, 1763.

I turned on the pillow with a little moan, and at this juncture Jeeves entered with the vital oolong. I clutched at it like a drowning man at a straw hat.

P.G. Wodehouse, *Right Ho, Jeeves* (1934).

I decided absolutely against Bournemouth. It was symbolic that I couldn't even get China tea there.

Arnold Bennett, diary entry, 31 December, 1909.

I left Miss Matty with a good heart. Her sales of tea during the first two days had surpassed my most sanguine expectations. The whole country round seemed to be all out of tea at once. The only alteration I could have desired in Miss Matty's way of doing business was, that she should not have so plaintively entreated some of her customers not to buy green tea – running it down as a slow poison, sure to destroy the nerves, and produce all manner of evil. Their pertinacity in taking it, in spite of all her warnings, distressed her so much that I really thought she would relinquish the sale of it, and so lose half her custom; and I was driven to my wits' end for instances of longevity entirely attributable to a persevering use of green tea. But the final argument, which settled the question, was a happy reference of mine to the train-oil and tallow candles which the Esquimaux not only enjoy but digest. After that she acknowledged that 'one man's meat might be another man's poison,' and contented herself thenceforward with an occasional remonstrance when she thought the purchaser was too young and innocent to be acquainted with the evil effects green tea produced on some constitutions, and an habitual sigh when people old enough to choose more wisely would prefer it.

Elizabeth Gaskell, *Cranford* (1853).

She murmured something and offered him coffee.

'I never drink it. It's poison. I'll have tea though, if you have good tea, not that American mould in teabags.'

Marilyn French, *The Women's Room* (1978).

The trouble with tea is that originally it was quite a good drink. So a group of the most eminent British scientists put their heads together, and made complicated biological experiments to find a way of spoiling it. To the eternal glory of British science their labour bore fruit. They suggested that if you do not drink it clear, or with lemon or rum and sugar, but pour a few drops of cold milk into it, and no sugar at all, the desired object is achieved. Once this refreshing, aromatic, oriental beverage was successfully transformed into colourless and tasteless gargling-water, it suddenly became the national drink of Great Britain and Ireland – still retaining, indeed usurping, the high-sounding title of tea.

George Mikes, *How to be an Alien* (1946).

A dreadful controversy has broken out in Bath, whether tea is most effectually sweetened by lump or pounded sugar; and the worst passions of the human mind are called in to action by the pulversists and the lumpists. I have been pressed by ladies on both sides to speak in favour of their respective theories, at the Royal Institution, which I have promised to do.

Sidney Smith, quoted by Hesketh Pearson in *The Smith of Smiths* (1934).

I have just partaken of that saddest of things – a cup of *weak* tea. Oh, why must it be weak! How much more pathetic is it to hear someone say as she puts it down before you: 'I am afraid it is rather weak.' One feels such a brute to take advantage of it until it is a little stronger. I grasp the cup; it seems to quiver – to breathe 'coward!' I confess, I can never hear a person at a tea party say (in that timid whisper you know, as though they were shamefully conscious): '*very* weak for me, please' without wanting to burst into tears. Not that I like desperately strong tea – No, let it be moderate strength, tea that rings the bell. Very strong tea does seem to give you your penny back – in the teapot from the taste of it.

Katherine Mansfield, diary entry, December, 1920.

What is the Latin for tea? What! Is there no Latin word for tea? Upon my soul, if I had known that I would have let the vulgar stuff alone.

Hilaire Belloc, 'On Tea' (1908).

'Pour it back in the mule' is what I say about tea.

Andrea Levy, *Small Island* (2004).

'Unhappy speculation around the subject of coffee'

I breakfast on delicious Indian tea. Coffee and China tea are intolerable at breakfast time, and for me, coffee unless it is very good and made by somebody else is pretty intolerable at any time. It seems to me an inconvenient and much over-rated drink, but this I will admit to be matter of personal taste.

Iris Murdoch, *The Sea, The Sea* (1978).

The morning cup of coffee has an exhilaration about it which the cheering influence of the afternoon or evening cup of tea cannot be expected to reproduce.

Oliver Wendell Holmes, *Over the Teacups* (1891).

A cup of coffee – real coffee – home brewed, home-ground, home made, that comes to you dark as a hazel-eye, but changes to a golden bronze as you temper it with cream that never cheated, but was real cream from its birth, thick, tenderly yellow, perfectly sweet, neither lumpy nor frothing on the Java: such a cup of coffee is a match for twenty blue devils and will exorcise them all.

Henry Ward Beecher, *Eyes and Ears* (1862).

For a South Indian, of all worries the least tolerable is coffee worry. Coffee worry may be defined as all unhappy speculation around the subject of coffee, as a habit, its supplies, its price, its quality, its morality, ethics, economics and so on. For a coffee addict (he does not like to be called an addict, the word has a disparaging sense, he feels that we might as well call each other milk addicts or food addicts or air addicts), the most painful experience is to hear a tea-drinker or a cocoa-drinker or a purist who drinks only water hold forth on the evils of drinking coffee. He views it as an attack on his liberty of thought and action. Even a misquoted Parliament report (as it recently happened) on the coffee policy of the government can produce in him the gravest disturbance, temporarily though.

It is not right to call it a habit. The word 'habit' like the word 'addict' has a disparaging sense. One might call smoking a habit, one might call almost everything else a habit, but not coffee. It is not a habit; it is a stabilising force in human existence achieved through a long evolutionary process. The good coffee, brown and fragrant, is not a product achieved in a day. It is something attained after laborious trails and errors. At the beginning people must have attempted to draw decoction from the raw seed itself or tried to chew it; and then they learnt to fry it, and in the first instance, nearly converted it into charcoal. Now people have developed a sixth sense, and know exactly when the seed should be taken out of the frying pan and ground. Nothing pleases a normal man of South India more than the remark, 'Oh, the coffee in his house is excellent. You cannot get the like of it anywhere else in the world.' Conversely no one likes to hear that his coffee is bad, although the truth may be that the powder he has used is adulterated, the strainer has let in all the powder, and there is every indication that they have (a horrible thing to do) added jaggery to the decoction. In this instance the thing to appreciate is not the coffee itself but the spirit behind it.

South India has attained world renown for its coffee and every South Indian jealously guards this reputation.

Coffee forms nearly thirty per cent of any normal family budget. The South Indian does not mind this sacrifice. He may beg or run into debt for the sake of coffee, but he cannot feel that he has acquitted himself in his worldly existence properly unless he is able to provide his dependents with two doses of coffee a day and also ask any visitor who may drop in, 'Will you have coffee?' without fear at heart. This is the basic minimum for a happy and satisfied existence. Here and there we may see households where the practice is more elaborately organized, and where coffee has to be available all hours of day or night. There are persons who call for a cup of coffee before starting a fresh sentence while writing. Perhaps all this may be too much. These are likely to come under the category of addicts, but their constant demand is understandable. No man asks for a fresh cup of coffee without criticizing the previous one. 'It was not quite hot . . . it seemed to have too much sugar. Let me see now this is . . .' It is only a continuous search for perfection, and let no one spoil it by giving it a bad name. Anyway, it cannot be called an addiction since anything that takes on that name brings forth evil results. Coffee has produced no bad result. It is supposed to spoil sleep, but there is a considerably growing school of thought that it is very good for insomnia. For one person who may say that coffee keeps him awake there are now at least three to declare that they can have a restful night only when they have taken a cup before retiring. All moralizing against coffee has misfired in this part of the country. 'Coffee is a deadly poison, you are gradually destroying your system with it, etc.' declares some purist. He may lecture form a public platform or on a street corner but people will listen to him with only a pitying tolerance, with an air of saying, 'Poor fellow, you don't know what you are talking about, you don't know what you are missing. You will still live and learn.' In course of time this prophecy is fulfilled. Many a man who came to scoff has remained to pray. Coffee has many conquests: saints, philosophers, thinkers and artists, who can never leave the bed unless they learn that coffee is ready, but not the least of its conquest is among those who came to wage a war on it.

R.K. Narayan, 'Coffee Worries' (1956).

Handing her son the plate of cookies, Miss Beryl shooed him out of the kitchen, then searched out the instant coffee in a remote cupboard. It took her a few minutes to boil the water, arrange the coffee cups on a tray, compose herself and return to the living room, where the Joyce woman was brushing cookie crumbs from her ample bosom. The plate was empty.

'Mmmm,' the woman cooed when she sipped her coffee. 'I'm sorry to be such trouble, but *honestly*, if I have decaffeinated after five, I'm up *all night long*!'

And then she was off again, explaining how she had always *adored* coffee, had always drunk twenty cups a day and never had any problems until recently. But now, *Lord*, it was simply *tragic* what coffee did to her. There was no other *word* for it besides tragic, but wasn't that the way with all the good things, the things you *really loved*. Everything good was either immoral or fattening, she added, apropos of nothing, and then cackled as if the cleverness of this observation were attributable to herself.

While the woman talked, Miss Beryl sank comfortably into her seat and tried not to glare, taking what solace there was in the fact that the coffee she'd given her guest was not decaf. Slender consolation, since the fool woman was probably wrong about caffeine as she was about everything else. Thinking she'd drunk decaf, she'd sleep like the dead.

Richard Russo, *Nobody's Fool* (1993).

The best proof that tea or coffee are favourable to intellectual expression is that all nations use one or the other as aids to conversation.

Philip Gilbert Hamerton, *The Intellectual Life* (1873).

In Europe the most obstreperous nations are those most addicted to coffee. Coffee produced the Fascisti of Italy, and excited the French to the madness of the Ruhr. We rightly speak of a storm in a teacup as the tiniest disturbance in the world, but out of a coffee-cup come great hurricanes.

Robert Lynd, 'Afternoon Tea' (1923).

3. LOCAL DELICACIES

'Roast beef and snails'

The dislike which France, until, let us say 1909, bore for England, was summed up in two words of withering reproach, 'Roast beef'. The contempt which, until 1909, every healthy Englishman felt for French superiority in art, literature, and music, found its outlet, and perhaps its appeasement, by shouting 'frogs' at them, by shouting 'snails'.

Harold Nicolson, 'Food' (1942).

What passes for cookery in England is an abomination (they agreed). It is putting cabbages in water. It is roasting meat till it is like leather. It is cutting off delicious skins of vegetables. 'In which,' said Mr Bankes, 'all the virtue of the vegetable is contained.' And the waste, said Mrs Ramsay. A whole French family could live on what an English cook throws away.

Virginia Woolf, *To the Lighthouse* (1927).

The great in France live very magnificently, but the rest very miserably. There is no happy middle state as in England. The shops of Paris are mean; the meat is such as would be sent to a gaol in England: and Mr Thrale justly observed, that the cookery of the French was forced upon them by necessity: for they could not eat their meat, unless they added some taste to it.

James Boswell, *Life of Johnson* (1791).

Like wine, steak is in France a basic element, nationalised even more than socialised. It figures in all the surroundings of alimentary life: flat, edged with yellow, like the sole of a shoe, in cheap restaurants; thick and juicy in the bistros which specialise in it; cubic, with the core of all moist throughout beneath a light charred curst, in haute cuisine. It is a part of all the rhythms, that of the comfortable meal and that of the bachelor's bohemian snack. It is food at once expeditious and dense, it effects the best possible ratio between economy and efficacy, between mythology and its multifarious ways of being consumed.

Roland Barthes, 'Steak and Chips' (1992).

I was seated at a table covered with all those good things which the land of France produces for the delectation of *gourmets*. I was eating a *pâté de Chartres*, which is alone sufficient to make one love one's country.

Anatole France, *The Crime of Sylvestre Bonnard* (1881).

I am always pleased when I dine with an old Gentleman in Berkshire, who has the true Spirit of a Briton; for being, from a natural Love to his Country, a Lover of Beef and Pudding, he has it for a constant Sunday Dinner, which he Pleasantly terms a Protestant Meal. Tho' he is a Man naturally sparing of Discourse, he is very lavish in the Praises of Sir Loin, and as satirical on French Soups and Fricasees, which Popish Cookery, he maintains, is an Emblem of the Popish Religion, a Gallimafry, a Hotch Potch of no one knows what; and therefore like a good Subject and good Christian, wishes People of Fashion would reform their Taste, and eat more consistent with their Loyalty to their King and Security to the Church by Law established.

'Gluttony', *The Universal Spectator* (1736).

Of their cookery, there is but one opinion; for every man in Europe that can afford a great table, either keeps a French cook, or one instructed in the same manner. That is far beyond our own, I have no doubt in asserting. We have about half-a-dozen real English dishes, that exceed anything, in my opinion, to be met with in France; by English dishes I mean, a turbot and lobster sauce; ham and chicken; turtle; a haunch of venison; a turkey and oysters; and after these, there is an end of an English table. It is an idle prejudice to class roast beef among them; for there is not better beef in the world than at Paris. Large handsome pieces were almost constantly on the considerable tables I have dined at. The variety given by their cooks, to the same thing, is astonishing; they dress an hundred dishes in an hundred different ways, and most of them excellent; and all sorts of vegetables have a savouriness and flavour, from rich sauces, that are absolutely wanted to our greens boiled in water.

Arthur Young, 'On French Cooking' (1789).

As a specimen of French auberge cookery, I cannot help serving up a dish of spinage to you, as it was served to me at this house. We came in early in the afternoon, and while I was in the court-yard I saw a flat basket stand upon the ground, the bottom of which was covered with boiled spinage; and as my dog, and several others in the yard, had often put their noses into it, I concluded it was put down for *their* food, not *mine*, till I saw a dirty girl patting it up into round balls; and two children, the eldest not above three years old, slavering in, and playing with it, one of whom, *to lose no time*, was performing *an office* that none could *do for her*. I asked the maid what she was about, and what is was she was so preparing! For I began to think I had been mistaken, till she told me it was spinage; – 'not for me, I hope,' said I, – '*oui, pour vous et le monde.*' I then forbad her bringing any to table; and putting the little girl off her centre, by an angry push, made her almost as dirty as the spinage; and I could perceive her mother, the hostess, and some French travellers who were near, looked upon me as a brute for *disturbing la pauvre enfant*; nevertheless, with my *entrée* came up a dish of this *delicate spinage*, with which I made the girl a very pretty *Châpeau Anglois*, for I turned it, dish and all, upon her head.

Philip Thicknesse, 'A Dish of Delicate Spinage' (1775).

'Experts on regional cooking'

It is commonly said, even by the English themselves, that English cooking is the worst in the world. It is supposed to be not merely incompetent, but also imitative, and I read quite recently, in a book by a French writer, the remark: 'The best English cooking is, of course, simply French cooking.'

Now that is simply not true. As anyone who has lived long abroad will know, there is a whole host of delicacies which it is quite impossible to obtain outside the English-speaking countries. No doubt the list could be added to, but here are some of the things that I myself have sought for in foreign countries and failed to find.

First of all, kippers, Yorkshire pudding, Devonshire cream, muffins and crumpets. Then a list of puddings, that would be interminable if I gave it in full: I will pick out for special mention Christmas pudding, treacle tart and apple dumplings. Then an almost equally long list of cakes: for instance, dark plum cake (such as you used to get at Buzzard's before the war), short-bread and saffron buns. Also innumerable kinds of biscuit, which exist, of course, elsewhere, but are generally admitted to be better and crisper in England.

Then there are the various ways of cooking potatoes that are peculiar to our own country. Where else do you see potatoes roasted under joint, which is far and away the best way of cooking them? Or the delicious potato cakes that you get in the north of England? And it is far better to cook new potatoes in the English way – that is, boiled with mint and then served with a little melted butter or margarine – than to fry them as is done in most countries.

Then there are the various sauces peculiar to England. For instance, bread sauce, horse-radish sauce, mint sauce and apple sauce, not to mention redcurrant jelly, which is excellent with mutton as well as with hare, and various kinds of sweet pickle, which we seem to have in greater profusion than most countries.

What else? Outside these islands I have never seen a haggis, except one that came out of a tin, nor Dublin prawns, nor Oxford marmalade, nor several other kinds of jam (marrow jam and bramble jelly, for instance), nor sausages of quite the same kind as ours.

Then there are the English cheeses. There are not many of them but I fancy that Stilton is the best cheese of its type in the world, with Wensleydale not far behind. English apples are also outstandingly good, particularly the Cox's Orange Pippin.

And finally, I would like to put in a word for English bread. All the bread is good, from the enormous Jewish loaves flavoured with caraway seeds to the Russian rye bread which is the colour of black treacle. Still, if there is anything quite as good as the soft part of the crust from an English cottage loaf (how soon shall we be seeing cottage loaves again?) I do not know of it.

No doubt some of the things I have named above could be obtained in continental Europe, just as it is possible in London to obtain vodka or bird's nest soup. But they are all native to our shores, and over huge areas they are literally unheard of.

South of say, Brussels, I do not imagine that you would succeed in getting hold of a suet pudding. In French there is not even a word that exactly translates 'suet'. The French, also, never use mint in cookery and do not use black currants except as a basis of a drink.

It will be seen that we have no cause to be ashamed of our cookery, so far as originality goes or so far as the ingredients go. And yet it must be admitted that there is a serious snag from the foreign visitor's point of view. This is, that you practically don't find good English cooking outside a private house. If you want, say, a good, rich slice of Yorkshire pudding you are more likely to get it in the poorest English home than in a restaurant, which is where the visitor necessarily eats most of his meals.

It is a fact that restaurants which are distinctively English, and which also sell good food are very hard to find. Pubs, as a rule, sell no food at all, other than potato crisps and tasteless sandwiches. The expensive restaurants and hotels almost all imitate French cookery and write their menus in French, while if you want a good cheap meal you gravitate naturally toward a Greek, Italian or Chinese restaurant. We are not likely to succeed in attracting tourists while England is thought of as a country of bad food and unintelligible by-laws. At present one cannot do much about it, but sooner or later rationing will come to an end, and then will be the moment for our national cookery to revive. It is not a law of nature that every restaurant in England should be either foreign or bad, and the first step towards an improvement will be a less long-suffering attitude in the British public itself.

George Orwell, 'In Defence of English Cookery' (1943).

Now that we are upon the article of cookery, I must own, some of their dishes are savoury, and even delicate, but I am not yet Scotchman enough to relish their singed sheep's-head and haggice, which were provided at our request one day at Mr. Mitchelson's where we dined.

Tobias Smollett, *The Expedition of Humphrey Clinker* (1771).

He found Miss Bradwardine presiding over the tea and coffee, the table loaded with warm bread, both of flour, oatmeal and barley meal, in the shape of loaves, cakes, biscuits and other varieties, together with eggs, reindeer ham, mutton and beef ditto, smoked salmon, marmalade and all the other delicacies which induced even Johnson himself to extol the luxury of a Scotch breakfast above that of all other countries. A mess of oatmeal porridge, flanked by a silver jug, which held an equal mixture of cream and butter milk, was placed for the Baron's share of this repast.

Walter Scott, *Waverley* (1819).

MR MACQUEDY: Well, sir, and what do you say to a fine fresh trout, hot and fry in a napkin? or a herring out of the water into the frying pan, on the shore of Loch Fyne?

THE REV. DR. FOLLIOTT: Sir, I say every nation has some eximious virtues; and your country is pre-eminent in your glory of fish for breakfast. We have much to learn from you in that line.

Thomas Love Peacock, *Crochet Castle* (1831).

As for the leg of mutton, it is truly wonderful; nothing so good had I ever tasted in the shape of a leg of mutton. The leg of mutton in Wales beats the leg of mutton of any other country, and I have never tasted a Welsh leg of mutton before. Certainly I shall never forget the first Welsh leg of mutton which I tasted, rich but delicate, replete with juices deprived from the aromatic herbs of the noble Berwyn, cooked to a turn and weighing just four pounds.

George Borrow, *Wild Wales* (1862).

I carried two portions of fish and chips back to the room for Hortense and me. There she was, still sitting on the bed. Her face, even after this time, remained set in an ill-tempered frown. 'See here, Miss Mucky Foot,' I said. 'I have fish and chips for you and me.' Only her big eyes swivelled to my direction while her arms folded tighter across her chest. I got out two plates, which were neatly stacked in the cupboard. Unwrapping and placing the fish and chips on the plate I tell her, 'You know what the English do?' Of course she did not reply but I did not expect her to. 'They eat this food straight from the newspaper. No plate. Nothing.' I knew this high-class woman would not be able to keep her face solemn in the presence of such barbarity. Scandalised, she could not stop herself staring on me in disbelief. 'Yes from the newspaper!'

Andrea Levy, *Small Island* (2004).

Our father liked his food, but it had to be British. Suet pudding was one of his favourites, a yellow hill studded with raisins wrinkled as rocks, the sides sliced then slabbed with cold butter on to which sugar fell crunchy as snow. More sugar sifted on to the morning porridge, the crust of the apple pie, the Eccles cakes, the Bakewell tart. Food was treated like gentlemen callers in a Victorian novel; it was interrogated as to its intentions, its culture and origins. Paella, spaghetti and couscous were forbidden suitors at our door. No daughter of mine, our father seemed to imply, will keep company with a sweet potato, a mango, or yam.

Michèle Roberts, 'Les Menus Plaisirs' (2001).

It was largely due to him I discovered my immense interest in different foods, for not only did we travel to many countries to taste it, but his interest stimulated mine. He insisted that we ate the food of the country, even a sheep's eye in Arabia, a fearsome, huge object which I don't recommend.

Theodora Fitzgibbon, *With Love* (1982).

Dish succeeded dish in bewildering opulence, set down between us, in great straw containers usually. There were no forks. We thrust with our hands into odorous hills of couscous, or with our fingers stripped delicate ribbons of fish from the bones. But the *chef-d'oeuvre* was a dish of mutton and whole onions, stewed in honey. I repeat: stewed in honey. It was celestial. If you are sceptical, go to Morocco for yourself; try it and you will believe.

Louis Golding, 'There Were No Table Napkins' (1972).

Now we have heard how Mrs. Sedley had prepared a fine curry for her son, just as he liked it, and in the course of dinner a portion of this dish was offered to Rebecca.

'What is it?' said she, turning an appealing look to Mr. Joseph.

'Capital,' said he. His mouth was full of it: his face quite red with the delightful exercise of gobbling. 'Mother, it's as good as my own curries in India.'

'Oh, I must try some, if it is an Indian dish,' said Miss Rebecca. 'I am sure everything must be good that comes from there.'

'Give Miss Sharp some curry, my dear,' said Mr. Sedley, laughing.

Rebecca had never tasted the dish before.

'Do you find it as good as everything else from India?' said Mr. Sedley.

'Oh, excellent!' said Rebecca, who was suffering tortures with the cayenne pepper.

'Try a chili with it, Miss Sharp,' said Joseph, really interested.

'A chili,' said Rebecca, gasping. 'Oh yes!' She thought a chili was something cool, as its name imported, and was served with some. 'How fresh and green they look,' she said, and put one into her mouth. It was hotter than the curry;

flesh and blood could bear it no longer. She laid down her fork. 'Water, for Heaven's sake, water!' she cried.

William Makepeace Thackeray, *Vanity Fair* (1847).

Upon the second table was a lobster, rather shattered and dissected, but still a lobster. There was a large dish of black potatoes, which were in fact truffles, the very largest truffles which the most expert of the Perigord trufflers had been able to unearth. Pink hog-like noses rootling for truffles: careful and experienced Perigourdins selecting the ones, those round bumpy ones which my particular millionaire was known to like. Then there were scarlet pepperheads from Thessaly, and pickled cucumbers from the Ukraine, spices from Bali and Sumatra, a little silver nutmeg-grater, a little gold instrument for crushing picatilloes, a little crystal mortar for grinding those locarto beans which come from Marakesh; the roots of a palmetto mush; olives from Ithaca.

Harold Nicolson, 'Food' (1942).

The best part of Germany was the food. There was a richness and spiciness about it that we missed in England. We liked the rye bread, the black honey (black, I believe, because it came from the combs of the previous year), the huge ice-cream puddings made with fresh raspberry juice, and the venison, and the honey cakes, and the pastries, and particularly the sauces made with different sorts of mushrooms. And the bretzels, and carrots cooked with sugar, and summer pudding made of cranberries and blue-berries.

Robert Graves, *Goodbye to all That* (1929).

Every advent, we entered the purgatory of *lutefisk*, a repulsive gelatinous fishlike dish that tasted of soap and gave off an odour that would gag a goat. We did this in honour of our Norwegian ancestors, much as if the survivors of a famine might celebrate their deliverance by feasting on elm bark. I always felt the cold creeps as Advent approached, knowing that this dread delicacy would be put before me and I'd be told, 'Just have a little.' Eating 'a little' was, like vomiting 'a little', as bad as 'a lot.'

Garrison Keillor, *Lake Wobegon Days* (1985).

The Chinese food arrives. Delicious saliva fills his mouth. He really hasn't had any since Texas. He loves this food that contains no disgusting proofs of slain animals, a bloody slab of cow haunch, a hen's sinewy skeleton; these ghosts have been minced and destroyed and painlessly merged with the shapes of unfeeling vegetables, plump green bodies that invite his appetite's innocent gusto. Candy. Heaped on a smoking breast of rice. Each is given such a tidy hot breast, and Margaret is in a special hurry to muddle hers with glazed chunks; all eat well. Their faces take colour and strength from the oval plates of dark pork, sugar peas, chicken, stiff sweet sauce, shrimp, water chestnuts, who knows what else.

John Updike, *Rabbit, Run* (1960).

The food they sold, certainly wholesome, nutritious, colourful, even tasty in its way, had been researched by Chen. It bore no resemblance at all to Chinese cuisine. They served from a stereotyped menu, similar to those outside countless other establishments in the UK. The food was, if nothing else, thought Lily, provenly successful: English tastebuds must be as degraded as the care of their parents; it could, of course, be part of a scheme of cosmic repercussion. 'Sweet and sour pork' was their staple, naturally: batter musket balls encasing a tiny core of meat, laced with a scarlet sauce that had an interesting effect on the urine of the customer the next day. Chen knew because he tried some and almost fainted the morning after, fearing some frightful internal haemorrhaging (had Lily been making him overdo it lately?) and going round with a slight limp until the mid-afternoon when the stream issued as clear as ever.

Timothy Mo, *Sour Sweet* (1982).

The greatest Chinese cook I ever met was named Henry Hong – at least the Chinese I knew told me he was the greatest cook, for I never ate any of his handiwork.

'North China cook not much,' said Henry Hong. 'Shanghai cook different, not much. Nobody Canton, Hankow, beat me.

'When we see Eulopean eat steak,' he said, 'we think there go one half-civilize. He know he hungry; no know make utensil for cook, burn meat on piece fire.'

I thought him an arrogant fellow, like most experts on regional cooking.

A.J. Liebling, *Back Where I Came From* (1938).

'102 per cent American'

This Joel Duffle suggests that the contest consist of twelve courses of strictly American food, each side to be allowed to pick six dishes, doing the picking in rotation, and specifying the weight and quantity of the course selected to any amount the contestant making the pick desires, and each course is to be divided for eating exactly in half, and after Miss Violette Shumberger and Nicely-Nicely whisper together a while, they say the terms are quite satisfactory.

The Horsey tosses a coin for the first pick, and Joel Duffle says heads, and it is heads, and he chooses, as the first course, two quarts of ripe olives, twelve bunches of celery, and four pounds of shelled nuts, all this to be split fifty-fifty between them. Miss Violette Shumberger names twelve dozen cherry-stone clams as the second course, and Joel Duffle says two gallon of Philadelphia pepper-pot soup as the third. Well, Miss Violette Shumberger and Nicely-Nicely whisper together again and Violette puts in two five-pound striped bass, the heads and tails not to count in the eating, and Joel Duffle names a twenty-two pound roast turkey. Each vegetable is rated as one course, and Miss Violette Shumberger asks for twelve pounds of mashed potatoes with brown gravy. Joel Duffle says two dozen ears of corn of the cob, and Violette replies with two quarts of lime beans. Joel Duffle calls for twelve bunches of asparagus cooked in butter, and Violette mention ten pounds of stewed new peas. This gets them down to the salad, and it is Joel Duffle's play, so he says six pound of mixed green salad with vinegar and oil dressing, and now Miss Violette Shumberger has the final selection, which is dessert. She says it is a pumpkin pie, two feet across, and not less than three inches deep.

Damon Runyon, 'A Piece of Pie' (1950).

The trouble with American cooking, Harald said, was the dearth of imagination in it and the terrible fear of innards and garlic. He put garlic in everything and was accounted quite a cook.

Mary McCarthy, *The Group* (1963).

There's an old joke. Uh, two elderly women are at a Catskills mountain resort, and one of 'em says: 'Boy, the food at this place is really terrible.' The other one says, 'Yeah, I know, and such small portions.'

Woody Allen, *Annie Hall* (1977).

If you are going to America, bring your own food.

Fran Lebowitz, *Social Studies* (1977).

It is indeed very foolish, if one is English, or even American to be unduly patriotic about one's food. We have our virtues. The English have their bacon and their beef. The Americans have their salads and those crisp but flabby things one eats with treacle. But we have also our failures. It would be mere jingoism to contend that the halibut of the English dining-car is anything more than a dead and sodden fish. One would have to be 102 per cent American to defend those sickly and gaseous beverages with which, so I am told, the most powerful nation of the twentieth century destroys it teeth and its digestion.

Harold Nicolson, 'Food' (1942).

If it seemed too hot for Cracker Jacks, I might get a cold drink. Mr Sessions might have already stationed himself by the cold-drinks barrel, like a mind reader. Deep in ice water that looked black as ink, murky shapes that would come up as Coca-Cola, Orange Crushes, and various flavours of pop, were all swimming around together. When you gave the word, Mr Sessions plunged his bare arm in to the elbow and fished out your choice, first try. I favoured a locally bottled concoction called Lake's Celery. (What else could it be called? It was made by a Mr Lake out of celery. It was a popular drink here for years but not known universally, as I found out when I arrived in New York and ordered one at the Astor bar.) You drank on the premises, with feet set wide apart to miss the drip, and gave him back his bottle.

Eudora Welty, 'The Little Store' (1975).

The Dashiki Chief has distributed among them all the greatest grandest sweetest creamiest runniest and most luscious mess of All-American pop drinks, sweets, and fried food ever brought together in one place. Sixty strong, sixty loud, sixty wild, they come swinging into the great plush gold-and-marble lobby of the San Francisco City Hall with their hot dogs, tacos, Whammies, Frostees, Fudgsicles, french fries, Eskimo pies, Awful-Awfuls, Sugar-Daddies, Sugar Mommies, Sugar-Babies, chocolate-covered frozen bananas, malted milks, Yoo-Hoos, berry pies, bubble gums, cotton candy, Space Food sticks, Frescas, Baskin-Robbins boysen-berry-cheesecake ice-cream cones, Milky Ways, M&Ms, Tootsie pops, Slurpees, Drumsticks, jelly doughnuts, taffy apples, buttered Karamel Korn, root-beer floats, Hi-C punches, large Cokes, 7-Ups, Three Musketeer bars, frozen Kool-Aids – with the Dashiki Chief in the vanguard.

Tom Wolfe, *Mau-Mauing the Flak Catchers* (1970).

'The whole Mediterranean'

The whole Mediterranean, the sculpture, the palms, the gold beads, the bearded heroes, the wine, the ideas, the ships, the moonlight, the winged gorgons, the bronze men, the philosophers – all of it seems to rise in the sour, pungent taste of these black olives between the teeth. A taste older than meat, older than wine. A taste as old as cold water.

Lawrence Durrell, *Prospero's Cell* (1945).

How dearly I should like to return to Spain and eat my way northward from Seville to Madrid, then to gnaw steadily through the Castiles and chew on to the Basque country, and so to pass, slowly and appreciatively, devouring like a cater-pillar, through the Asturias into Galicia.

H.V. Morton, *A Stranger in Spain* (1955).

Several stages lower in the list came the vegetarian dishes – *olla gitana, ropa vieja* or old clothes, lentil and bean pottages, string beans with eggs, various sorts of omelettes, and at the very bottom the national dish of Castile, which is known as *puchero*. This is a boiled affair, not unlike the French *pot-au-feu*, of which the essential ingredients are pork, chunks of *tocino* or bacon fat, potatoes, turnips, and chick peas. The chick pea, from which Cicero took his name, is a yellow bullet which explodes in the inside into several cubic feet of gas, while if the cook knows her job properly she will see that the meat is boiled till it has no taste left and that the fat, a yellowish white in colour, is rancid. A Spaniard feels when he eats this dish that he has vindicated his toughness of fibre. He has not degenerated from the breed of men who conquered a continent with a handful of adventurers, wore hair-shirts day and night till they stuck to their flesh, and braved the mosquitoes of the Pilcomayo and the Amazon.

Gerald Brenan, *South from Granada* (1957).

The Spanish breakfast is as deplorable as the French: rings of batter fried in oil called *churros*, and a cup of coffee or chocolate. The result is that all morning Spaniards are nibbling shrimps, prawns, little bits of ham, anything they can get to stave off hunger until luncheon at two o'clock.

H.V. Morton, *A Stranger in Spain* (1955).

On my last day in Marseilles I treated myself to a bouillabaisse, the dish that Marseilles gave to the world. The fish broth was pungent and flavourful, saffron-coloured as in the classic recipe, presented with croutons and cheese and rémoulade and potatoes. And the vital ingredients were the fruit of the Mediterranean – rouget (mullet), rascasse (red, spiny hog-fish found only in the Mediterranean), Saint-Pierre (John Dory), moules, whiting, monkfish, bass, gurnet,

weever, conger eel, crawfish, clams.The crab was very small.
The waiter lifted the shell with a fork.

'And this, as they say in English, you suck.'

Paul Theroux, *The Pillars of Hercules* (1995).

The near end of the street was rather dark, and had mostly
vegetable shops. Abundance of vegetables – piles of white
and green fennel, like celery, and great sheaves of young, pur-
plish, sea-dust-coloured artichokes, nodding their buds, piles
of big radishes, scarlet and bluey purple, carrots, long strings
of dried figs, mountains of big oranges, scarlet large peppers,
a last slice of pumpkin, a great mass of colours and vegetable
freshness. A mountain of black-purple cauliflowers, like nig-
gers' heads, and a mountain of snow-white ones next to
them. How the dark, greasy, night-stricken street seems to
beam with these vegetables, all this fresh delicate flesh of
luminous vegetables piled there in the air, and in the recesses
of the windowless little caverns of the shops, and gleaming
forth on the dark air, under the lamps. The q-b at once wants
to buy vegetables. 'Look! Look at the snow white broccoli.
Look at the huge finocchi. Why don't we get them? I *must*
have some. Look at those great clusters of dates – ten francs a
kilo, and we pay sixteen. It's monstrous. Our place is simply
monstrous' . . . However, and however, it is seven o'clock and
the shops are beginning to shut. No more shop-gazing. Only
one lovely place: raw ham, boiled ham, chickens in aspic,
chicken vol-au-vents, sweet curds, curd cheese, rustic cheesecake, smoked sausages, beautiful fresh mortadella, huge
Mediterranean red lobsters, and those lobsters without
claws. 'So good! So good!' we stand and cry it aloud.

D.H. Lawrence, *Sea and Sardinia* (1923).

In Greece, where the food stands or falls according to the
quality of the oil, we had eaten *avgolemoa*, delicious rich,

spiced soup with oriental affiliations made with chicken, rice, eggs and lemon and served with black pepper, etc., etc.; in Turkey, where the vegetables were the freshest and the meat the best almost anywhere in the Mediterranean, we had allowed ourselves to be fooled into eating *kadin budu*, lady's thighs, which turned out to be pastry and good old unerotic meat croquettes; in Israel we had eaten chickens' testicles and bulls' testicles, described on the menu as 'eggs of adult ox in extent'; and elsewhere in Israel, *kreplach* made with chopped meat and dumplings, and so many *blintzes*, *knishes*, *bagels* and helpings of lox that I imagined myself back on Broadway; and in Egypt we had been treated to a meal which took what seemed an eternity to materialize, consisting of *ful*, dried brown beans cooked with red lentils incredibly slowly over a low charcoal fire, eaten with chicken cooked with the aromatic *mulukhia* plant and prickly pears, not all of which had been adequately de-pricked.

Eric Newby, *On the Shores of the Mediterranean* (1984).

One doctor enrolled Desdemona in a longevity study. He was writing an article for a medical journal on 'The Mediterranean Diet'. To that end he plied Desdemona with questions about the cuisine of her homeland. How much yoghurt had she consumed as a child? How much olive oil? Garlic? She answered every one of his queries because she thought his interest indicated that there was something, at last, organically, the matter with her, and because she never missed a chance to stroll through the precincts of her childhood. The doctor's name was Müller. German by blood, he renounced his race when it came to its cooking. With postwar guilt, he decried bratwurst, sauerbraten, and Königsberger Klopse as dishes verging on poison. They were the Hitler of foods. Instead he looked to our Greek diet – our eggplant aswim in tomato sauce, our cucumber dressings and fish-egg spreads, or *pilafi*, raisins and figs – as potential curatives, as life-giving, artery cleansing, skin-smoothing wonder drugs. And what Dr Müller said appeared to be true: though he was only forty-two, his face was wrinkled, burdened with jowls. Gray hair prickled up the sides of his head; whereas my father, at forty-eight, despite the coffee stains beneath his eyes, was still the possessor of an unlined olive complexion and a rich, glossy, black head of hair. They didn't call it Grecian Formula for nothing. It was in our food! A veritable fountain of youth in our dolmades and tarama salata and even in our baklava, which didn't commit the sin of containing refined sugar but had only honey. Dr Müller showed us graphs he'd made, listing the names and birth dates of Italians, Greeks, and a Bulgarian living in the Detroit metropolitan area, and we saw our entrant – Desdemona Staphanides, age ninety-one – going strong in the midst of the rest. Plotted against Poles killed off by kielbasa, or Belgians done in by pommes frites, or Anglo-Saxons disappeared by puddings, or Spaniards stopped cold by chorizo, our Greek dotted line kept going where theirs tailed off in a tangle of downward trajectories. Who knew?

Jeffrey Eugenides, *Middlesex* (2002).

4. SHOPPING AND COOKING

'Vast halls gleaming with treasure'

She liked me run errands for her, walk to a near farm to fetch a recipe or take a present of vegetables. She liked me to feed the dogs, clean out their kennels, help with the cow. But best of all was when she told me to go down to the vegetable garden.

I took two large baskets, smelling of herbs, from the hooks in the pantry, and walked off from the front of the house by myself: the dogs always went with Bob. It was a sandy winding path between musasa trees, a mile or so. Half-way to the garden, a hundred yards off in the trees, were granite boulders, where the python lived. Anywhere near those rocks, when with Bob, the dogs were called to heel, and he had his rifle read on the slope of his arm. 'A python can move as fast as a horse,' said he. 'A dog, that's what they like best. A python got poor Wolf, two years ago.' I always walked slowly past that ominous pile, looking hard for the python. I saw it once, a grey coil, motionless in dappled light, easy to mistake for granite. My feet took me off in a spasm of terror as fast as I could go down to the garden, though I would have to return . . . delicious terror, because I did not believe the python was interested in me. There were pythons on our farm and we often saw them, and I had never been chased by a snake speeding through the grasses. They were always sliding off as fast as they could go.

I stopped before reaching the garden, and stood sniffing that air soaked with herbs, tomatoes, the clean smell of peas. The garden was a half acre fenced to keep the duiker out, but baboons sometimes got in and threw aubergines and green peppers around, and made holes where they dug potatoes. The tomatoes sent out a smell so strong it made me giddy. A row of them, yards long, of plants as tall as a man, weighted with green tomatoes, yellow tomatoes, green tomatoes red-streaked which I sometimes had to pick for chutney – and so many ripe tomatoes there was no hope of ever picking even half of them. I filled the baskets with these dead ripe, heavy, aromatic, scarlet tomatoes, added bunches of thyme and parsley from beds crammed full of herbs, and went out, carefully fastening the gate. As I left the birds descended from the trees, and even the sky, where they had been waiting for me to leave, commenting in their various tongues on this interruption of their feasting. Some of the tomatoes had been hollowed out by their beaks, and peapods had been opened and bright green peas rolled about the paths. Joan said, 'We don't grow food for ourselves, we are a charitable institution,' and Bob said, 'Birds and animals have to live too.'

I walked slowly back up the long path, feeling the heat get to me, and the tomatoes dragged my arms down. I did not run now as I passed the python's territory, though I watched the grasses for a rippling movement that meant he was coming for me. Slowly I went on, listening to the birds, the birds of Africa, and particularly the doves, the slow sleepy sound seducing you into daydreams and longing.

I put the baskets side by side on the kitchen table, and drank glass after glass of tepid water from the filter. 'Just make us some soup for lunch,' Joan called from the veranda where she reposed on a long grass chair, another beside her loaded with cats. I filled the grate of the Carron Dover stove, the same as ours – the same as everyone's then – fitting the wood in there so there were proper spaces for air, and soon the fire was going. From a hook over the stove I lifted down an enormous black iron pot that always smelled of herbs no matter how much it was washed. Into the pot I emptied baskets of tomatoes, twenty pounds or more. The pot was set over the flames, and I went to the back veranda and sat there, legs dangling, watching the wandering fowls, the dogs, if they were there, the cats, whose lives were parallel to the dogs, neither taking notice of the other. Cats had their own chairs, places, bushes, where they waited out the long heat of the day. Dogs flopped about on the veranda, but never in the house, which was Joan's territory and the cats'.

After an hour or so I took the pot off the stove. It was now filled with a gently bubbling red pulp. Stirring it with a wooden spoon in one hand, I fished out bits of skin with a silver spoon in the other. This was a slow pleasurable process. When all the tight little rolls of pink skin were out, in went salt, pepper, a handful of thyme and about a quart of yellow cream. This simmered for another hour.

Then, lunch. Platefuls of reddish, scented brew, making your head reel with its smell. I did not eat it so much as absorb it, together with thoughts of the vegetable garden where by now hundreds of birds would be drinking from the water buckets, or fluffing themselves in the dust between the beds. The doves' long slow cooing, the tomato reek, the python – all this became part of the taste.

That's tomato soup. Never accept anything less.

Doris Lessing, *Under My Skin* (1994).

Françoise, rejoicing in the opportunity to devote herself to that art of cooking at which she was so gifted, stimulated, moreover, by the prospect of a new guest, and knowing that she would have to compose, by methods known to her alone, a dish of *Boeuf à la gelée*, had been living in the effervescence of creation; since she attached the utmost importance to the intrinsic quality of the materials which were to enter into the fabric of her work, she had gone herself to the Halles to procure the best cuts of rump-steak, shin of beef, calves'-feet, just as Michelangelo spent eight months in the mountains of Carrara choosing the most perfect blocks of marble for the monument of Julius II.

Marcel Proust, *The Remembrance of Things Past* (1913).

Having rekindled the fire, she thought she would go to market while the water heated. The walk revived her spirits, and flattering herself that she had made good bargains, she trudged home again after buying a very young lobster, some very old asparagus, and two boxes of acid strawberries.

Louisa May Alcott, *Little Women* (1868).

Whatever you may think of the matter, it is no such easy thing to keep house for two people. A man cannot always live on sheep's heads, and liver and lights, like the lions in the Tower; and a joint of meat, in so small a family, is an endless encumbrance. My butcher's bill for last week amounted to four shillings and tenpence. I set off with a leg of lamb, and was forced to give part of it away to my washerwoman. Then I made an experiment upon a sheep's heart, and that was too little. Next I put three pounds of beef into a pie, and this had like to have been too much, for it lasted three days, though my landlord was admitted to share in it. Then as to small beer, I am puzzled to pieces about it. I have bought as much for a shilling as will serve us at least a month, and it is grown sour already. In short, I never know how to pity poor housekeepers before; but now I cease to wonder at that politic cast which their occupation usually gives to their countenance, for it is really a matter full of complexity.

William Cowper, letter to Joseph Hill, 3 July, 1765.

The bread I eat in London, is a deleterious paste, mixed up with chalk, alum, and bone-ashes; insipid to the taste, and destructive to the constitution. The good people are not ignorant of this adulteration; but they prefer it to wholesome bread, because it is whiter than the meal of corn: thus they sacrifice their taste and their health, and the lives of their families, in order to live by his profession. The same monstrous depravity appears in their veal, which is bleached by repeated bleedings, and other villainous arts, till there is not a drop of juice left in the body, and the poor animal is paralytic before it dies; so void of all taste, nourishment, and savour, that a man might dine as comfortably on a white fricassee of kidskin gloves, or chip hats from Leghorn. As they have discharged the natural colour from their bread, their butcher's-meat, and poultry, their cutlets, ragouts, fricassees, and sauces of all kinds; so they insist upon having the complexion of their pot-herbs mended, even at the hazard of their lives. Perhaps, you will hardly believe they can be so mad as to boil their greens with brass half-pence, in order to improve their colour; and yet nothing is more true – Indeed, without this improvement in the colour, they have no personal merit. They are produced in an artificial soil, and taste of nothing but the dunghills, from whence they spring. My cabbage, cauliflower, and 'sparagus in the country, are as much superior in flavour to those that are sold in Covent Garden, as my heath-mutton is to that of St. James's market; which in fact, is neither lamb nor mutton, but something betwixt the two, gorged in the rank fens of Lincoln and Essex, pale, coarse, and frowzy – As for the pork, it is an abominable carnivorous animal, fed with horse-flesh and distillers' grains; and the poultry is all rotten, in consequence of a fever, occasioned by the infamous practice of sewing up the gut, that they may be the sooner fattened in coops, in consequence of this cruel retention.

Of the fish, I need say nothing in this hot weather, but

that it comes sixty, seventy, fourscore, and a hundred miles by land-carriage; a circumstance sufficient, without any comment, to turn a Dutchman's stomach, even if his nose was not saluted in every alley with the sweet flavour of fresh mackerel, selling by retail – This is not the season for oysters; nevertheless, it may not be amiss to mention, that the right Colchester are kept in slime-pits, occasionally overflowed by the sea; and that the green colour, so much admired by voluptuaries of this metropolis, is occasioned by the vitriolic scum, which rises on the surface of the stagnant and stinking water – Our rabbits are bred and fed in the poulterer's cellar, where they have neither air not exercise, consequently they must be firm in flesh, and delicious in flavour; and there is no game to be had for love or money.

It must be owned, that Covent-garden affords some good fruit; which, however, is always engrossed by a few individuals of over-grown fortune, at an exorbitant price; so that little else than the refuse ·of the market falls to the share of the community; and that is distributed by such filthy hands, as I cannot look at without loathing. It was but yesterday that I saw a dirty barrow-bunter in the street, cleaning her dusty fruit with her own spittle; and, who knows but some fine lady of St. James's parish might admit into their delicate mouth those very cherries, which had been rolled and moistened between the filthy, and, perhaps, ulcerated chops of a St. Giles's huckster – I need not dwell on the pallid, contaminated mash, which they call strawberries; soiled and tossed by greasy paws through twenty baskets crusted with dirt; and then presented with the worst milk, thickened with the worst flour, into a bad likeness of cream: but the milk itself should not pass unanalysed, the produce of faded cabbage-leaves and sour draff, lowered with hot water, frothed with bruised snails, carried through the streets in open pails, exposed to foul rinsings, discharged from doors and windows, spittle, snot, and tobacco-quids from foot-passengers, overflowings from mud-carts, spatterings from coach-wheels, dirt and trash chucked into it by roguish boys for the joke's sake, the spewings of infants, who have slabbered in the tin-measure, which is thrown back in that condition among the milk, for the benefit of the next customer; and finally, the vermin that drops from the rags of the nasty drab that vends this precious mixture, under the respectable denomination of milk-maid.

Tobias Smollett, *The Expedition of Humphrey Clinker* (1771).

Each salesman tries his utmost to sell his wares, tempting the passers-by with his bargains. The boy with his stock of herbs offers 'a double 'andful of fine parsley for a penny'; the man with the donkey-cart filled with turnips has three lads to shout for him to their utmost, with their 'Ho! ho! hi-i-i! What do you think of this here? A penny a bunch – harrah for free trade! *Here's* your turnips!' Until it is seen and heard, we have no sense of the scramble that is going on throughout London for a living. The same scene takes place in Tottenham-court-road – the same in Whitecross-street; go to whatever corner of the metropolis you please, and there is the same shouting and the same struggling to get the penny profit out of the poor man's Sunday dinner.

Henry Mayhew, *London Labour and the London Poor* (1861–2).

Walking to Hanley this morning I was struck by the orange-apple *cold* Christmas smell of the greengrocers' shops.

Arnold Bennett, diary entry, 24 December, 1903.

London supermarkets these days are vast halls gleaming with treasure; even grubby old Holloway Road and Seven Sisters Road now have five between them, in which you can buy anything from anywhere in the world. The seasons no longer exist; time and space have been annihilated. Every whim can be satisfied, whether you want Korean red pepper paste and pickled cabbage, Mexican mole sauce of chocolate and spices, black pastaciutta dyed with squid ink, sesame-scattered Turkish loaves of bread as round and thick as your arm, or sweetmeats from the Lebanon dusted with honey crystals and flecks of brilliant pistachio. You've only to tell me your desire and I'll provide you with whatever you want.

Michèle Roberts, 'The Cookery Lesson' (2001).

There was no smell of food here, no hint of the rich stew of odours you'd find in a Mexican market – these people sanitized their groceries just as they sanitized their kitchens and toilets and drove the life from everything, imprisoning their produce in jars and cans and plastic pouches, wrapping their meat and even their fish in cellophane – and yet still the sight and proximity of all these comestibles made his knees go weak again.

T. Coraghessan Boyle, *The Tortilla Curtain* (1995).

'A cook . . . for the occasion'

Cookery has become an art, a noble science; cooks are gentlemen.

Robert Burton, *Anatomy of Melancholy* (1621).

They had a *Cook* with them for the occasion,
To boil the chickens up with marrowbones,
Tart powdered flavouring, spiced with garlingale.
No better judge than he of London ale.
And he could roast and seethe and boil and fry,
Make a thick soup and bake a proper pie.

But to my mind it was the greatest shame
He'd got an open sore upon his shin;
For he made chicken-pudding with the best.

Geoffrey Chaucer, The Canterbury Tales (1380s).

Spitting in the omelette is fine revenge. Or overloading it with pepper. But take care not to masturbate into the mix, as someone in the next village did, sixty years ago. The eggs got pregnant. When he heated them they grew and grew, becoming quick and lumpy, until they could outwit him (and all his hungry guests waiting with beer and bread out in the yard) by leaping from the pan with their half-wings and running down the lane like boys.

Jim Crace, The Devil's Larder (2001).

Mrs Murphy's gastronomic skills were scanty. She was reckless in her use of fat which she poured over her food, straight from the pan, treating it as a sauce.

Caroline Blackwood, Corrigan (1984).

Look at Cody's mother – a nonfeeder, if ever there was one. Even back in his childhood, when they'd depended on her for nourishment . . . why, mention you were hungry and she'd suddenly act rushed and harassed, fretful, out of breath, distracted. He remembered her coming home from work in an evening and tearing irritably round the kitchen. Tins toppled out of the cupboards and fell all over her – pork 'n' beans, Spam, oily tuna fish, peas canned olive-drab. She cooked in her hat, most of the time. She whimpered when she burned things. She burned things you would not imagine it possible to burn and served other things half-raw, adding jarring extras of her own design such as crushed pineapple in the mashed potatoes. (Anything, as long as it was a leftover, might as well be dumped in the pan with anything else.) Her only gravy was Campbell's cream of mushroom soup, undiluted. And till Cody was grown, he had assumed that roast beef had to be stringy – not something you sliced, but a leathery dry object which you separated with a fork, one strand from the other, and dropped with a clunk on your plate.

Anne Tyler, *Dinner at the Homesick Restaurant* (1982).

At midnight Mary worked in the chaotic kitchen. There was a hot yellow glare like the blaze of ripe butter. She cooked in colours. One meal consisted of haddock, chicken-skin (astutely preserved by Mary from the previous day), and swede darkened with the blood of beetroots; another of liver, grapes, kidney-beans and the outer leaves of artichokes. She cooked everything until it was the right colour.

Martin Amis, *Other People: A Mystery Story* (1981).

She turned her attention to the lemon sauce for the veal. Another floating speck; she tried to skim it off. Examined the carrots. Not good.

'What is it?' Marion asked, peering into the serving dishes.

'I'm afraid,' Frances said, 'the fucking Saudiflon is coming off the pans.'

Marion picked up a spoon and began to stab and scrape at the vegetables, her tongue between her teeth.

'You can't do that,' Frances said. 'We'll be here all night.'

'Slosh some more butter on. They'll never know.'

'That'll just make it float about on top.'

'Well, never mind,' Marion said. 'I'll bring the salad, shall I? I don't suppose Saudiflon tastes of anything. With luck they'll just think it's black pepper.'

Hilary Mantel, *Eight Months on Ghazzah Street* (1988).

Home to dinner; and there I took occasion, from the blackness of the meat as it came out of the pot, to fall out with my wife and the maids for their sluttery; and so left the table.

Samuel Pepys, diary entry, 22 December, 1661.

One night, my then seventeen-year-old brother had gone down into the kitchen to make himself a late-night snack. He found some hot-dogs in the refrigerator. Not wanting to wait for water to boil, he got out a frying pan. Next he decided to cut the hot dogs in half. 'I wanted to increase the surface area,' he explained to me later. Rather than slicing the hot dogs lengthwise, Chapter Eleven tried various combinations to amuse himself. He made notches here and slits there and then he put all the hot dogs in a pan and watched what happened.

Not much, that first night. But a few of my brother's incisions resulted in the hot dogs assuming funny shapes. After that, it became a kind of game with him. He grew adept at manipulating the shapes of cooking hot dogs and, for fun, developed an entire line of gag frankfurters. There was the hot dog that stood on end when heated, resembling the Tower of Pisa. In honour of the moon landing, there was the Apollo 11, whose skin gradually stretched until, bursting, the wiener appeared to blast off into the air.

Jeffrey Eugenides, *Middlesex* (2002).

Lily told us an absurd, hilarious story about Carl, furious at Lily's cooking, deciding he would make potato pancakes the way his mother did, spilling batter on the stove, where it stuck, and in a rage, throwing the whole bowl across the kitchen saying it was her job anyway, and storming out of the house to eat at McDonald's, and leaving her with the mess, the kids to be fed and bathed, both of them crying at the failure of Daddy's boasted dinner and at the shock, the noise, and confusion.

Marilyn French, *The Women's Room* (1978).

The whole circle of her joyful friends would be there, and she meant to give them to eat of the famous dish of lobster *à la Riseholme* . . . It had already produced a great deal of wild surmise in the minds of the housewives at Tilling, for no one could conjecture how it was made, and Lucia had been deaf to all requests for the recipe: Elizabeth had asked her twice to give it to her, but Lucia had merely changed the subject without attempt at transition: she had merely talked about something quite different. This secretiveness was considered unamiable for the use of Tilling was to impart its culinary mysteries to friends, so that they might enjoy their favourite dishes at each other's houses, and lobster *à la Riseholme* had long been an agonizing problem to Elizabeth. She had made an attempt at it herself, but the result was not encouraging. She had told Diva and the Padre that she felt sure she had 'guessed it', and, when bidden to come to lunch and partake of it, they had both anticipated a great treat. But Elizabeth had clearly guessed wrong, for lobster *à la Riseholme à la Mapp* had been found to consist of something resembling lumps of India-rubber (so tough that the teeth positively bounced from them on contact) swimming in a dubious pink gruel, and both of them left a great deal on their plates, concealed as far as possible under their knives and forks, though their hostess continued manfully to chew, till her jaw muscles gave out.

E.F. Benson, *Mapp and Lucia* (1935).

'I bet you cook good, huh? Darlene asked.

'Mother doesn't cook,' Ignatius said dogmatically. 'She burns.'

'I used to cook too when I was married,' Darlene told them. 'I sort of used a lot of that canned stuff, though. I like that Spanish rice they got and that spaghetti with the tomato gravy.'

'Canned food is a perversion,' Ignatius said. 'I suspect that it is ultimately very damaging to the soul.'

'Lord, my elbow's starting up again,' Mrs Reilly sighed.

'Please. I am speaking,' her son told her. 'I never eat canned food. I did once, and I could feel my intestines starting to atrophy.'

John Kennedy Toole, *A Confederacy of Dunces* (1980).

The British cook, for her iniquities, is a foolish woman who should be turned into a pillar of salt which she never knows how to use.

Oscar Wilde, 'Dinners and Dishes' (1885).

I bought horsemeat when available, but sometimes after queuing for an hour there would be only bones left, so I made a stew of them with flour dumplings: I did get whale meat twice which was much appreciated: when I tasted it once, I found it extremely rich. Ends of bread were baked in the oven and sometimes when there would be nothing else, she ate those with made-up dried milk powder and a few drops of cod liver oil.

Theodora Fitzgibbon, *With Love* (1982).

It was my mother who could accomplish anything, who herself had to admit that it might even be that she was actually too good . . . she could make jello, for instance, with sliced peaches hanging in it, peaches just suspended there, in defiance of the law of gravity. She could bake a cake that tasted like a banana. Weeping, suffering, she grated her own horseradish, rather than buy the pishachs they sold in a bottle at the delicatessen. She watched the butcher, as she put it, 'like a hawk', to be certain that he did not forget to put her chopped meat through the kosher grinder.

Philip Roth, *Portnoy's Complaint* (1969).

I know a happily married woman who is a brilliant cook and has always used garlic. One day she overdid it and her husband, who claimed as so many people do that he detested it, asked in horror if there was garlic in the food. The wife kept her head and instead of scoring a point by saying that he had been eating it for twelve years said, yes, she had just tried some but wouldn't do so again. She is still happily married, the husband is still eating garlic and still thinks very rightly that his wife is an inspired cook.

Rupert Croft-Cooke, *English Cooking: A New Approach* (1960).

Kay was glad when Harald tooled home (that was one of his favourite expressions) for dinner, instead of eating with the others in that speak-easy. Once he had brought one of the authors, and Kay had made a salmon loaf with cream pickle sauce. That would have to be the night they broke for dinner early, and there was quite a wait (Bake 1 hour, the recipe went, and Kay usually added fifteen minutes to what the cookbook said), which they had to gloss over with cocktails. Harald did not realise what a rush it was for her, every day now, coming home from work at Mr Macy's and having to stop at Gristede's for the groceries; Harald never had time any more to do the marketing in the morning. And, strange to say, every since *she* had started doing it, it had become a bone of contention between them. He liked A & P because it was cheaper, and she liked Gristede's because they delivered and had fancy vegetables – the Sutton Place trade, Harald called it. Then Harald liked to cook the same old stand-bys (like his spaghetti with dried mushrooms and tomato paste), and she liked to read the cookbook and the food columns and always be trying something new. He said she had no imagination, following recipes with her glasses on and measuring the seasoning and timing every thing: cooking was a lively art and she made it academic and lifeless.

Mary McCarthy, *The Group* (1963).

My own Miss Fellows had been cook in some very good places, but you would never have guessed it had you seen her walking along to do her shopping in Shepherd's Market. She was not stout, red-faced and blousy as one expects a cook to be; she was spare and very upright, neatly but fashionably dressed, a woman of middle age with determined features; her lips were rouged and she wore an eyeglass. She was businesslike, quiet, coolly cynical and very expensive.

W. Somerset Maugham, *Cakes and Ale* (1930).

She convection-roasted country ribs to brownness and cut them thin, along the grain, for presentation, reduced and darkened the kraut gravy to bring out its nutty, earthy, cabbage, porky flavour, and tarted up the plate with twin testicular new potatoes, a cluster of Brussels sprouts, and a spoon of stewed white beans that she lightly spiked with roasted garlic. She invented luxurious new white sausages. She matched a fennel relish, roasted potatoes, and good bitter wholesome rapini with fabulous pork chops that she bought direct from a sixties holdover organic farmer who did his own butchering and made his own deliveries. She took the guy to lunch and visited his farm in Lancaster County and met the hogs in question, examined their eclectic diet (boiled yams and chicken wings, acorns and chestnuts) and toured the sound proofed room where they were slaughtered. She extracted commitments from her old crew at Mare Scuro. She took former colleagues out on Brian's AmEx and sized up the local competition (most of it reassuringly undistinguished) and sampled desserts to see if anybody's pasty chef was worth stealing. She staged one-woman late-night forcemeat festivals. She made it with red cabbage and with shredded kale in cabbage juice, with juniper berries and black peppercorns. She hurried along the fermentation with hundred-watt bulbs.

Jonathan Franzen, *The Corrections* (2001).

Anyone who tells a lie has not a pure heart and cannot make good soup.

Ludwig van Beethoven, quoted by Ludwig Nolh in
Beethoven as Depicted by his Contemporaries (1880).

'A combined operation'

The anniversary happened to fall on a Monday which was a bit of luck, for Gervaise could count on the Sunday afternoon for starting the cooking. On Saturday in the shop, while the women were rushing through their work, there was a long parliament to settle finally what they would have. Only one item had been agreed upon for three weeks, that was a fat roast goose. As they talked about it their eyes goggled with greed. The goose had even been bought, and Ma Coupeau fetched it out so that Clémence and Madame Putois could feel the width of it. There were exclamations about how enormous it seemed, with its coarse skin all distended with yellow fat.

'Soup to start with?' said Gervaise. 'Some soup and a little piece of boiled beef always goes down well, doesn't it? . . . Then we should want something with a sauce.'

Clémence suggested rabbit, but no, you never seemed to eat anything else, and everybody was fed up with rabbit. Gervaise visualized something more out of the common, and when Madame Putois mentioned blanquette of veal they all looked at each other with broadening smiles. That was an idea, nothing would make such an effect as a blanquette of veal.

'After that,' Gervaise went on, 'we should have to have something else with sauce.'

Ma Coupeau wondered about fish, but the others made a face at this and banged harder with their irons. No, nobody liked fish; it didn't agree with you and it was full of bones. Boss-eyed Augustine ventured to say that she loved skate, but Clémence shut her up with a sock on the jaw. Finally, when the boss had hit on stewed chine of pork with potatoes, and a fresh smile had spread over all faces, Virginie blew in like a tornado, her face aflame.

'You've just come at the right moment,' said Gervaise. 'Ma Coupeau, let her see the bird.' . . .

'Well, now, and what about a veg?'

'Why not peas and bacon?' said Virginie. 'I could live on nothing but that.'

'Yes, yes, peas and bacon?' agreed all the others, whilst Augustine, transported, thrust her poker deep into the stove.

By three o'clock on the Sunday afternoon Ma Coupeau had lit the two stoves belonging to the house and a third earthenware one borrowed from the Boches. At half past three the stew was bubbling away in a big saucepan lent by the nearby restaurant, their own being considered too small. It had been decided to cook the blanquette of veal and the chine of pork the day before because those dishes are better hotted up, only they wouldn't do the cream sauce until just before sitting down to the meal. That would still leave a lot of work for Monday – the soup, the peas and bacon and the roast goose. The back room was all ablaze with the three ovens, brown sauce was sizzling in the pans with a pungent smell of burnt flour, whilst the big stewpan puffed jets of steam like a boiler, its sides shaken by deep and solemn rumblings. Ma Coupeau and Gervaise, with white aprons tied on, filled the room as they bustled about, taking off parsley stalks, looking for the salt and pepper and turning the meat with a wooden spoon. They had sent Coupeau off to get him out of the way, but still they had people round their necks all the afternoon. The smells of cooking in the house were so good that women came down one after the other and found excuses for coming in simply to discover what was being cooked; and there they took root and waited until the laundress was obliged to lift off the lids.

Emile Zola, *L'Assommoir* (1876).

'There we are to breakfast; and while the good *fermière* makes the café au lait in a caldron, you and five others, whom I shall select, will spread with butter half a hundred rolls.'

Having formed his troop into line once more, he marched us straight on the farm, which, on seeing our force, surrendered without capitulation.

Clean knives and plates and fresh butter being provided, half a dozen of us, chosen by our professor, set to work under his directions to prepare for breakfast a huge basket of rolls, with which the baker had been ordered to provision the farm, in anticipation of our coming. Coffee and chocolate were already made hot; cream and new-laid eggs were added to the treat; and M. Emanuel, always generous, would have given a large order for *jambon* and *confitures* in addition, but that some of us, who presumed perhaps upon our influence, insisted that it would be a most reckless waste of victual. He railed at us for our pains, terming us '*des ménagères avares;*' but we let him talk, and managed the economy of the repast our own way.

Charlotte Brontë, *Villette* (1853).

The next day, Sunday 8 September, there was no gas to cook the breakfast with, so in a combined operation we made toast and coffee over an electric fire lying on its back, and cooked kippers on the flat part of an electric iron. For some time after this we smelt strongly of fish when we pressed our clothes, but at least we ate that day.

Theodora Fitzgibbon, *With Love* (1982).

There was a gridiron in the pantry, on which my morning rasher of bacon was cooked. We had it in, in a twinkling, and immediately applied ourselves to carrying Mr Micawber's idea into effect. The division of labour to which he had referred was this: – Traddles cut the mutton into slices; Mr Micawber (who could do anything of this sort to perfection) covered them with pepper, mustard, salt and cayenne; I put them on the gridiron, turned them with a fork, and took them off, under Mr Micawber's direction; and Mrs Micawber heated, and continually stirred, some mushroom ketchup in a little saucepan. When we had slices enough done to begin upon, we fell-to, with our sleeves still tucked up at the wrist, more slices sputtering and blazing on the fire, and our attention divided between the mutton on our plates, and the mutton then preparing.

Charles Dickens, *David Copperfield* (1850).

George gathered wood and made a fire, and Harris and I started to peel the potatoes. I should never have thought that peeling potatoes was such an undertaking. The job turned out to be the biggest thing of its kind that I had ever been in. We began cheerfully, one might almost say skittishly, but our light-heartedness was gone by the time the first potato was finished. The more we peeled, the more peel there seemed to be left on; by the time we had got all the peel off and all the eyes out, there was no potato left – at least none worth speaking of. George came and he had a look at it – it was about the size of a peanut. He said:

'Oh, that won't do! You're wasting them. You must scrape them.'

So we scraped them, and that was harder work than peeling. They are such an extraordinary shape, potatoes – all bumps and warts and hollows. We worked steadily for five-and-twenty minutes, and did four potatoes. Then we struck. We said we should require the rest of the evening for scraping ourselves.

I never saw such thing as potato-scraping for making a fellow in a mess. It seemed difficult to believe that the potato-scrapings in which Harris and I stood half-smothered, could have come off four potatoes. It shows you what can be done with economy and care.

George said that it was absurd to have only four potatoes in an Irish stew, so we washed half a dozen or so more, and put them in without peeling. We also put in a cabbage and about half a peck of peas. George stirred it all up, and then he said that there seemed to be a lot of room to spare, so we over-hauled the hampers, and picked out all the odds and ends and the remnants, and added them to the stew. There were half a pork pie and a bit of cold boiled bacon left, and we put them in. Then George found half a tin of potted salmon, and he emptied that into the pot.

He said that was the advantage of Irish stew: you got rid of such a lot of things. I fished out a couple of eggs that had got cracked, and we put those in. George said they would thicken the gravy.

I forgot the other ingredients, but I know nothing was wasted; and I remember that, towards the end, Montmorency, who had evinced great interest in the proceedings throughout, strolled away with an earnest and thoughtful air, reappearing, a few minutes afterwards, with a dead water-rat in his mouth, which he evidently wished to present as his contribution to the dinner; whether in a sarcastic spirit, or with a genuine desire to assist, I cannot say.

We had a discussion as to whether the rat should go in or not. Harris said that he thought it would be all right, mixed up with the other things, and that every little helped; but George stood up for precedent. He said he had never heard of water-rats in Irish stew, and he would rather be on the safe side, and not try experiments.

Harris said:

'If you never try a new thing, how can you tell what it's like? It's men such as you that hamper the world's progress. Think of the man who first tried German sausage!'

It was a great success, the Irish stew. I don't think I ever enjoyed a meal more. There was something so fresh and piquant about it. One's palate gets so tired of the old hackneyed things: here was a dish with a new flavour, with a taste like nothing else on earth.

And it was nourishing, too. As George said, there was good stuff in it. The peas and potatoes might have been a bit softer, but we all had good teeth, so that did not matter much: and as for the gravy, it was a poem – a little too rich, perhaps, for a weak stomach, but nutritious.

Jerome K. Jerome, *Three Men in a Boat* (1889).

5. MEALS

'A nourishing meal'

Being almost famished with hunger, having not eaten a morsel for some hours before I left the ship, I found the demands of nature so strong upon me, that I could not forbear showing my impatience (perhaps against the strict rules of decency) by putting my finger frequently to my mouth, to signify that I wanted food. The Hurgo (for so they call a great lord, as I afterwards learnt) understood me very well. He descended from the stage, and commanded that several ladders should be applied to my sides, on which above a hundred of the inhabitants mounted and walked towards my mouth, laden with baskets full of meat, which had been provided and sent thither by the king's orders, upon the first intelligence he received of me. I observed there was the flesh of several animals, but could not distinguish them by the taste. There were shoulders, legs, and loins, shaped like those of mutton, and very well dressed, but smaller than the wings of a lark. I ate them by two or three at a mouthful, and took three loaves at a time, about the bigness of musket bullets. They supplied me as fast as they could, showing a thousand marks of wonder and astonishment at my bulk and appetite. I then made another sign, that I wanted drink. They found by my eating that a small quantity would not suffice me; and being a most ingenious people, they slung up, with great dexterity, one of their largest hogsheads, then rolled it towards my hand, and beat out the top; I drank it off at a draught, which I might well do, for it did not hold half a pint, and

tasted like a small wine of Burgundy, but much more delicious. They brought me a second hogshead, which I drank in
the same manner, and made signs for more; but they had
none to give me.

Jonathan Swift, Gulliver's Travels (1726).

Presently we sat down to an immense meal of lung hash,
black bread, malt coffee and boiled potatoes. In the first reck-
lessness of having so much money to spend (I had given her
ten marks in advance for the week's board) Frau Nowak had
prepared enough potatoes for a dozen people. She kept shov-
elling them on to my plate from a big saucepan, until I
thought I should suffocate:

'Have some more, Herr Christoph. You're eating nothing.'

'I've never eaten so much in my whole life, Frau Nowak.'

'Christoph doesn't like our food,' said Herr Novak. 'Never
mind, Christoph, you'll get used to it.'

Christopher Isherwood, Goodbye to Berlin (1935).

Miss Vavasour, so assiduous in other areas of her care of
us, is capricious, not to say cavalier, in the matter not only of
luncheon but of meals in general, and dinner especially at
the Cedars can be a unpredictable refection. Anything might
appear on the table, and does. Tonight for instance she
served us breakfast kippers with poached eggs and boiled
cabbage. The Colonel, sniffing, ostentatiously wielded his
condiment bottles turn and turn about like a spot-the-pea
artist. To these wordless protests of his Miss Vavasour's
response is invariably one of aristocratic absent-mindedness
verging on disdain. After the kippers there were tinned pears
lodged in a gritty grey lukewarm substance which if childhood memory serves I think was semolina. Semolina, my
goodness. As we made our way through this stodge, with
nothing but the clicking of cutlery to disturb the silence, I

had a sudden image of myself as a sort of large dark simian something slumped there at the table, or not a something but a nothing.

John Banville, The Sea (2005).

They began with a soup square, which Leonard had just dissolved in some hot water. It was followed by the tongue – a freckled cylinder of meat, with a little jelly at the top, and a great deal of yellow fat at the bottom – ending with another square dissolved in water (jelly: pineapple), which Leonard had prepared earlier in the day. Jacky ate contentedly enough, occasionally looking at her man with those anxious eyes, to which nothing else in her appearance corresponded, and which yet seemed to mirror her soul. And Leonard managed to convince his stomach that it was having a nourishing meal.

E.M. Forster, Howard's End (1910).

Shukhov pulled his spoon out of his boot. His little treasure. It had been with him his whole time in the North, he'd cast it with his own hands out of aluminium wire and it was embossed with the words 'Ust-Izhma 1944'.

Then he removed his hat from his clean shaven head – however cold it might be, he could never bring himself to eat with this hat on – and stirred the cold skilly, taking a quick look to see what kind of helping they'd given him. An average one. They hadn't ladled it from the top of the cauldron, but they hadn't ladled it from the bottom either . . . The only good thing about skilly was that it was hot, but Shukhov's portion had grown quite cold. However, he ate it with his usual slow concentration. No need to hurry, not even for a house on fire. Sleep apart, the only time a prisoner lives for himself is ten minutes in the morning at breakfast, five minutes over dinner and five at supper.

The skilly was the same every day. Its composition depended on the kind of vegetable provided that winter. Nothing but salted carrots last year, which meant from September to June the skilly was plain carrot. This year it was black cabbage. The most nourishing time of the year was June: then all vegetables came to an end and were replaced by groats. The worst time was July; then they shredded nettles into the pot.

The little fish were more bone than flesh; the flesh had been boiled off the bone and had disintegrated, leaving a few remnants on head and tail. Without neglecting a single fish-scale or particle of flesh on the brittle skeleton, Shukhov went on champing his teeth and sucking the bones, spitting the remains on the table. He ate everything – the gills, the tail, the eyes when they were still in their sockets but not when they'd been boiled out and floated in the bowl separately – great fish eyes! Not then. The others laughed at him for that.

This morning Shukhov economized. As he hadn't returned to the hut he hadn't drawn his rations, so he ate his breakfast without bread. He'd eat the bread later. Might even be better that way.

After the skilly there was magara porridge. It had grown cold too, and had set into a solid lump. Shukhov broke it up into pieces. It wasn't only that the porridge was cold – it was tasteless when hot, and left you no sense of having filled your belly. Just grass, except that it was yellow, and looked like millet. They'd got the idea of serving it instead of cereals from the Chinese, it was said. When boiled, a bowlful of it weighed nearly a pound. Not much of a porridge but that was what it passed for.

Licking his spoon and tucking it back into his boot, Shukhov put on his hat and went to the sick-bay.

Alexander Solzhenitsyn, *One Day in the Life of Ivan Denisovich* (1962).

I could not help wondering in my own mind, as I contemplated the boiled leg of mutton before me, previous to carving it, how it came to pass that our joints of meat were of such extraordinary shapes – and whether our butcher contracted for all the deformed sheep that came into the world; but I kept my reflections to myself.

'My love,' said I to Dora, 'what have you got in that dish?'

I could not imagine why Dora had been making tempting little faces at me, as if she wanted to kiss me.

'Oysters, dear,' said Dora, timidly.

'Was that *your* thought?' said I, delighted.

'Ye-yes, Doady,' said Dora.

'There never was a happier one!' I exclaimed, laying down the carving-knife and fork. 'There is nothing Traddles like so much!'

'Ye-yes, Doady,' said Dora, 'and so I bought a beautiful little barrel of them, and the man said they were very good. But I – I am afraid there's something the matter with them. They don't seem right.' Here Dora shook her head, and diamonds twinkled in her eyes.

'They are only opened in both shells,' said I. 'Take the top one off, my love.'

'But it won't come off,' said Dora, trying very hard, and looking very much distressed.

'Do you know Copperfield,' said Traddles, cheerfully examining the dish, 'I think it is in consequence – they are capital oysters, but I *think* it is in consequence of their never having been opened.'

They never had been opened; and we had no oyster-knives – and couldn't have used them if we had; so we looked at the oysters and ate the mutton. At least we ate as much of it as was done, and made up with capers. If I had permitted him, I am satisfied that Traddles would have made a perfect savage of himself, and eaten a plateful of raw meat, to express enjoyment of the repast; but I would hear of no such immolation on the altar of friendship; and we had a course of bacon instead, there happening, by good fortune, to be cold bacon in the larder.

Charles Dickens, *David Copperfield* (1850).

'Our morning's repast'

He always made his own breakfast. Being a man who rose early and had plenty of time he did not, as some miners do, drag his wife out of bed at six o'clock. At five, sometimes earlier, he woke, got straight out of bed, and went downstairs. When she could not sleep, his wife lay waiting for this time, as for a period of peace. The only rest seemed to be when he was out of the house.

He went downstairs in his shirt and then struggled into the pit-trousers, which were left on the hearth to warm all night. There was always a fire because Mrs Morel raked. And the first sound in the house was the bang, bang of the poker against the raker, as Morel smashed the remainder of the coal to make the kettle, which was filled and left on the hob, finally boil. His cup and knife and fork, all he wanted except just the food, was laid ready on the table on a newspaper. Then he got his breakfast, made the tea, packed the bottom of the doors with rugs to shut out the draught, piled a big fire, and sat down to an hour of joy. He toasted his bacon on a fork and caught the drops of fat on his bread; then he put the rasher on his thick slice of bread, and cut off chunks with a clasp-knife, poured his tea into his saucer, and was happy. With his family about, meals were never so pleasant. He loathed a fork; it is a modern invention which has still scarcely reached common people. What Morel preferred was a clasp-knife. Then, in solitude, he ate and drank, often sitting, in cold weather, on a little stool with his back to the warm chimney-piece, his food on the fender, his cup on the hearth.

D.H. Lawrence, *Sons and Lovers* (1913).

The maltster, after having lain down in his clothes for a few hours, was now sitting beside a three-legged table, breakfasting of bread and bacon. This was eaten on the plateless system, which is performed by placing a slice of bread upon the table, the meat flat upon the bread, a mustard plaster upon the meat, and a pinch of salt upon the whole, then cutting them vertically downwards with a large pocket-knife till wood is reached, when the severed lump is impaled on the knife, elevated, and sent the proper way of food.

Thomas Hardy, *Far from the Madding Crowd* (1874).

Life, within doors, has few pleasanter prospects than a neatly arranged and well-provisioned breakfast table. We come to it freshly, in the dewy youth of the day, and when our spiritual and sensual elements are in better accord than at a later period; so that the material delights of the morning meal are capable of being fully enjoyed, without any very grievous reproaches, whether gastric or conscientious, for yielding even a trifle overmuch to the animal department of our nature.

Nathaniel Hawthorne, *The House of Seven Gables* (1851).

The following articles formed our morning's repast: one kit of boiled eggs, a second, full of butter; a third, full of cream; an entire cheese made of goat's milk; a large earthen pot, full of honey; the best part of a ham; a cold venison pastry; a bushel of oatmeal, made into thin cakes and bannocks, with a small wheaten loaf in the middle, for the strangers; a stone bottle full of whiskey, another of brandy, and a kilderkin of ale. There was a ladle chained to the cream kit, with curious wooden bickers to be filled from this reservoir. The spirits were drank out of a silver quaff, and the ale out of horns: a great justice was done to the collation by the guests in general; one of them in particular ate above two dozen of hard eggs, with a proportionable quantity of bread, butter, and honey; nor was one drop of liquor left upon the board.

Tobias Smollett, *The Expedition of Humphrey Clinker* (1771).

In about twenty minutes after I had ordered it, my breakfast made its appearance. A noble breakfast it was; such, indeed as I might have read of, but had never before seen. There was tea and coffee, a goodly white loaf and butter; there were a couple of eggs and two mutton chops. There was broiled and picked salmon – there was fried trout – there were also potted trout and potted shrimps. Mercy upon me! I had never previously seen such a breakfast set before me.

George Borrow, *Wild Wales* (1862).

The vapour of the boiled fish arose like incense from the shrine of a barbarian idol, while the fragrance of the Mocha might have gratified the nostrils of a tutelary Lar, or whatever power has scope over a modern breakfast table. Phoebe's Indian cakes were the sweetest offering of all – in their hue befitting the rustic altars of the innocent and golden age – or, so brightly yellow were they, resembling some of the bread which was changed to glistening gold when Midas tried to eat it. The butter must not be forgotten – butter which Phoebe herself had churned, in her own rural home, and brought it to her cousin as a propitiatory gift – smelling of clover blossoms, and diffusing the charm of pastoral scenery throughout the dark-panelled parlour. All this, with the quaint gorgeousness of the old china cups and saucers, and the crested spoons, and a silver cream jug (Hepzibah's only other article of plate, and shaped like the rudest porringer), set out a board at which the stateliest of old Colonel Pyncheon's guests need not have scorned to take his place. But the Puritan's face scowled down out of the picture, as if nothing on the table pleased his appetite.

Nathaniel Hawthorne, *The House of Seven Gables* (1851).

The tea consumed was the very best, the coffee the very blackest, the cream the very thickest; there was dry toast and buttered toast, muffins and crumpets; hot bread and cold bread, white bread and brown bread, home-made bread and baker's bread, wheaten bread and oaten bread, and if there be other breads than these, they were there; there were eggs in napkins, and crispy bits of bacon under silver covers; and there were little fishes in a little box, and devilled kidneys frizzling on a hot-water dish; which, by the bye, were placed closely contiguous to the plate of the worthy archdeacon himself. Over and above this, on a snow-white napkin, spread upon the sideboard, was a huge ham and a huge sirloin; the latter having laden the dinner-table on the previous evening. Such was the ordinary fare at Plumstead Episcopi.

Anthony Trollope, *The Warden* (1855).

For breakfast I had exactly what I fancied: two fat croissants with apricot jam, a piece of baguette with butter and Camembert, a bunch of muscat grapes, and several cups of black coffee with sugar. I consumed this feast very slowly while lying in bed. I'd laid the tray with an antique Quimper cup and saucer and plate. I'd put a vase of pink sweet peas on the nearby chest of drawers, clean sheets on the bed. I'd put on my new nightdress, eau-de-nil silk with pencil shoulder-straps. I was celebrating the start of my new life. I was not going to be half-hearted about it. I was going to do it properly.

Michèle Roberts, 'Taking It Easy' (1994).

I try to fix her a nice breakfast, because this sometimes improves her disposition, which is generally terrible. One morning not long ago, when I brought her a tray she clapped her hands to her face and began to cry. I looked at the tray to see if there was anything wrong. It was a nice breakfast – two hard boiled eggs, a piece of Danish, and a Coca-Cola spiked with gin. That's what she likes. I've never learned to cook bacon. The eggs looked alright and the dishes were clean, so I asked her what was the matter. She lifted her hands from her eyes – her face was wet with tears and her eyes were haggard – and said, in the Boysen-family accent, 'I cannot any longer endure being served breakfast in bed by a hairy man in his underwear.'

John Cheever, 'The Chimera' (1951).

'A bag lunch'

The special kids, the ones who wear keys around their necks, get to eat in the canteen. The canteen! Even the name sounds important. And these kids at lunch time go there because their mothers aren't home or home is too far away to get to.

My home isn't far but it's not close either, and somehow I got it into my head one day to ask my mother to make me a sandwich and write a note to the principal so I could eat in the canteen too.

Oh no, she says pointing the butter knife at me as if I'm starting trouble, no sir. Next thing you know everybody will be wanting a bag lunch – I'll be up all night cutting bread into little triangles, this one with mayonnaise, this one with mustard, no pickles on mine, but mustard on one side please. You kids just like to invent more work for me.

Sandra Cisneros, *The House on Mango Street* (1992).

We'd been on a school trip to Chester Zoo earlier in the week. That meant everybody in their Sunday best, vying for who had the cleanest socks and the most impressive sandwiches. Canned drinks were our envy, since most of us had orange squash in our Tupperware pots. The Tupperware always heated up, and burnt our mouths.

'You've got brown bread' (scuffling over the seats come three heads). 'What's that for? It's got bits in it, you vegetarian?'

I try not to take any notice as my sandwiches are prodded. The general sandwich inspection continues from seat to seat, alternating between murmurs of envy and shrieks of laughter. Susan Green had cold fish fingers in hers, because her family was very poor and had to eat leftovers even if they were horrible. Last time she'd only had brown sauce, because there weren't even any leftovers. The inspectorate decided that Shelley had the best. Bright white rolls stuffed with curried egg and a dash of parsley. And she had a can of lemonade.

Jeanette Winterson, *Oranges Are Not the Only Fruit* (1985).

The little girls of Avonlea school always pooled their lunches, and to eat three raspberry tarts all alone or even to share them only with one's best chum would have forever and ever branded as 'awful mean' the girl who did it. And yet, when the tarts were divided among ten girls you just got enough to tantalize you.

L.M. Montgomery, *Anne of Green Gables* (1908).

That noon, Ruby said she wanted to walk up and check on the apple orchard, so Ada suggested they have their lunch there. They made a picnic of the leftover pieces of last night's fried chicken, a small bowl of potato salad for which Ruby had whipped up the mayonnaise, and some vinegared cucumber slices. They carried the dinner up to the apple orchard in a wooden bucket and ate in under the trees on a quilt spread in the grass.

Charles Frazier, *Cold Mountain* (1997).

Our dinner in the harvest-field was always hot; none of your makeshift lumps of dough with onions stuffed into them: a dish known as Bedfordshire Clanger; no lumps of cold bacon and bread, no plain bread and cheese, no sandwiches. In one basket would repose a steak-and-kidney pie, perhaps, a rabbit pie, or a beef pudding, together with a basin of new potatoes, carrots, peas or beans: all wrapped in clean white napkins. In the other there would be, perhaps, an apple pie or, what I myself loved best of all, a pie of a small yellow local plum of extraordinarily good flavour and rather squarish in shape and touched with a faint blush of crimson, very like an apricot.

H.E. Bates, *An Autobiography* (2006).

I do not wish to describe the picnic party on top of the tower. You can imagine well enough what it is like to carve a chicken and tongue with a knife that has only one blade – and that snapped off short about half-way down. But it was done. Eating with your fingers is greasy and difficult – and paper dishes soon get to look very spotty and horrid. But one thing you can't imagine, and that is how soda-water behaves when you try and drink it straight out of a siphon – especially quite a full one. But if imagination will not help you, experience will, and you can easily try it for yourself if you can get a grown-up to give you the siphon. If you want to have a really thorough experience, put the tube in your mouth and press the handle very suddenly and very hard. You had better do it when you are alone – and out of doors is best for this experiment.

However you eat them, tongue and chicken and new bread

are very good things, and no-one minds being sprinkled with soda-water on a really fine day.

E. Nesbit, *Five Children and It* (1957).

'Hold hard a minute, then!' said the Rat. He looped the painter through a ring in his landing-stage, climbed up into this hole above, and after a short interval reappeared staggering under a fat, wicker luncheon-basket.

'Shove that under your feet,' he observed to the Mole, as he passed it down into the boat. Then he untied the painter and took the sculls again.

'What's inside it?' asked the Mole, wriggling with curiosity.

'There's cold chicken inside it,' replied the Rat briefly; 'coldtonguecoldhamcoldbeefpickledgherkinssaladfrenchrollscressandwidgespottedmeatgingerbeerlemonadesodawater—'

'O stop, stop,' cried the Mole in ecstasies: 'This is too much!'

'Do you really think so?' inquired the Rat seriously. 'It's only what I always take on these little excursions; and the other animals are always telling me that I'm a mean beast and cut it *very* fine.'

Kenneth Grahame, *The Wind in the Willows* (1908).

For lunch, he said, we could have biscuits, cold meat, bread and butter, and jam – but *no cheese*. Cheese, like oil, makes too much of itself. It wants the whole boat to itself. It goes through the hamper, and gives a cheesy flavour to everything else there. You can't tell whether you are eating apple pie, or German sausage, or strawberries and cream. It all seems cheese. There's too much odour about cheese.

Jerome K. Jerome, *Three Men in a Boat* (1889).

He untied his bundle, which consisted of three bunches of onions, and a great lump of Cheshire cheese wrapt up in a handkerchief; and taking some biscuit from the cupboard, fell to with a keen appetite, inviting us to share of the repast. – When he had fed heartily on this homely fare, he filled a large cup made of a cocoa-nut shell, with brandy, and drinking it off, told us, 'Prandy was the best menstruum for onion and sheese.'

Tobias Smollett, *The Adventures of Roderick Random* (1748).

She had skipped her lunch-hour, substituting a cheese-and-lettuce sandwich – a slice of plastic cheese between two pieces of solidified bubble-bath with several flaps of pallid greenery, brought in a cardboard carton by the restaurant take-out order boy – for real food.

Margaret Atwood, *The Edible Woman* (1969).

'The ceremony known as afternoon tea'

The fact remains, however, that the races which have a good breakfast have a bad luncheon and a bad dinner. Then we have buns for tea. Hot buttered buns and sometimes muffins. There will be no hope for Anglo-Saxon cooking until we train ourselves to have rusks and coffee for breakfast and no tea at all.

Harold Nicolson, 'Food' (1942).

Under certain circumstances there are few hours in life more agreeable than the hour dedicated to the ceremony known as afternoon tea. There are circumstances in which, whether you partake of the tea or not – some people of course never do, – the situation is in itself delightful.

Henry James, *The Portrait of a Lady* (1881).

In nothing is the English genius for domesticity more notably declared than in the institution of this festival – almost one may call it so – of afternoon tea. Beneath simple roofs, the hour of tea has something in it of sacred; for it marks the end of domestic work and worry, and the beginning of restful, sociable evening. The mere chink of cups and saucers tunes the mind to happy repose.

George Gissing, *The Private Papers of Henry Ryecroft* (1903).

A nice Scotch tea with good old silver spoons and admirable scones.

Arnold Bennett, diary entry, 5 January, 1905.

So Guster . . . prepares the little drawing-room for tea. All the furniture is shaken and dusted, the portraits of Mr and Mrs Snagsby are touched up with a wet cloth, the best tea-service is set forth, and there is excellent provision made of dainty new bread, crusty twists, cool fresh butter, thin slices of ham, tongue, and German sausage, and delicate little rows of anchovies nestling in parsley, not to mention new-laid eggs, to be brought up warm in a napkin, and hot buttered toast.

Charles Dickens, *Bleak House* (1853).

I was walking on when a maiden stood before me and looked. She had the greyest eyes.

'Would you,' she said, 'like a lobster?'

I observed her closely and realized that she was serious. Behind her lay in negligent attitudes dozens of lobsters on a table among roses. It was 4.30 p.m. It had never occurred to me that people eat lobster at tea-time. In fact, there is to my mind something almost indecent about it. I was so embarrassed that I said 'Yes', whereupon, giving me no time to repent, in the manner of women, she picked up a big scarlet brute and disappeared, leaving me to slink miserably to a chintz chair, with a clammy foreboding of great evil.

'Tea?' she asked.

I made a feeble protest, but she assured me that China tea 'goes' with lobster. I wanted to ask whether this experiment had ever been tried before by man, but was given no time. When the shell was empty some devil entered into me and urged me to reply 'Yes' to everything this girl said (and she was a good talker), with the result that basins of Dorset cream, pots of jam, puffy cakes oozing sweetness, ramparts of buns and crisp rolls became piled up behind the rose-bowl. The only thing I missed at this tea-party was the Mad Hatter.

H.V. Morton, 'Lobster Tea in Dorset' (1927).

'A dinner-party all to ourselves'

'Rat,' he moaned, 'how about your supper, you poor, cold, hungry, weary animal? I've nothing to give you – nothing – not a crumb!'

'What a fellow you are for giving in!' said the Rat reproachfully. 'Why, only just now I saw a sardine-opener on the kitchen dresser, quite distinctly; and everybody knows that means there are sardines about somewhere in the neigh-bourhood. Rouse yourself! Pull yourself together, and come with me and forage.'

They went and foraged accordingly, hunting through every cupboard and turned out every drawer. The result was not so very depressing after all, though of course it might have been better; a tin of sardines – a box of captain's biscuits, nearly full – and a German sausage encased in silver paper.

'There's a banquet for you!' observed the Rat, as he

arranged the table. 'I know some animals who would give their ears to be sitting down to supper with us to-night!'

Kenneth Grahame, *The Wind in the Willows* (1908).

'Let us have a dinner-party all to ourselves! May I ask you to bring up some herbs from the farm-garden to make a savoury omelette? Sage and thyme, mint and two onions, and some parsley. I will provide lard for the stuff-lard for the omelette,' said the hospitable gentleman with sandy whiskers.

Beatrix Potter, *The Tale of Jemima Puddleduck* (1908).

The tray was soon hoisted down, and before the merry chatter of cups and saucers began, the women disburdened themselves of their out-of-door things, and sent Mary upstairs with them. Then came a long whispering, and chinking of money, to which Mr and Mrs Wilson were too polite to attend; knowing, as they did full well, that it all related to the preparations for hospitality; hospitality that, in their turn, they should have such pleasure in offering. So they tried to be busily occupied with the children, and not to hear Mrs Barton's directions to Mary.

'Run, Mary dear, just round the corner, and get some fresh eggs at Tipping's (you may get one a-piece, that will be five-pence), and see if he has any nice ham cut, that he would let us have a pound of.'

'Say two pounds, missis, and don't be stingy,' chimed in the husband.

'Well a pound and a half, Mary. And get in Cumberland ham, for Wilson comes from there-a-way, and it will have a sort of relish of home with it he'll like, – and Mary' (seeing the lassie fain to be off) 'you must get a pennyworth of milk and a loaf of bread – mind you get it fresh and new – and, and – that's all, Mary.'

'No, it's not all,' said her husband. 'Thou must get sixpenny-worth of rum, to warm the tea; thou'll get it at the "Grapes". And thou just go to Alice Wilson; he says she lives just right round the corner, under 14, Barber Street' (this was addressed to his wife), 'and tell her to come and take her tea with us; she'll like to see her brother, I'll be bound, let alone Jane and the twins.'

'If she comes she must bring a tea-cup and saucer, for we have but half-a-dozen, and here's six of us,' said Mrs Barton.

'Pooh! Pooh! Jem and Mary can drink out of one surely.'

But Mary secretly determined to take care that Alice brought her tea-cup and saucer, if the alternative was to be her sharing any thing with Jem.

Elizabeth Gaskell, Mary Barton (1848).

When the mutton and an omelette, a samovar, vodka and some wine which the French had taken from a Russian cellar were brought in Ramballe invited Pierre to share his dinner, and himself immediately fell to, greedily and without delay attacking the viands like a healthy, hungry man, munching vigorously with his strong teeth, constantly smacking his lips, and exclaiming, 'Excellent! Delicious!' His face flushed and perspired. Pierre was hungry and glad to share the repast. Morel, the orderly, appeared with some hot water in a saucepan and placed a bottle of claret in it. He also fetched a bottle of kvass, taken from the kitchen for them to try. The French called it *limonade de cochon*, and Morel spoke well of the 'pigs' lemonade' he had found in the kitchen. But as the captain had the wine they had looted on their way across Moscow, he left the kvass to Morel and devoted himself to a bottle of Bordeaux. He wrapped a table-napkin round the neck of the bottle and poured out wine for himself and Pierre. Hunger appeased and the wine made the captain even more lively and he chatted non-stop all through dinner.

Leo Tolstoy, War and Peace (1869).

I did some more shopping and brought the ingredients of our supper round to his flat in Hampstead. It has taken me a long time to persuade Perry that it is stupid and immoral to go to expensive crowded restaurants to be served with bad food by contemptuous waiters and turned out before one is ready to go. As it was we had a long relaxed evening, ate a delicious curry (cooked by me, Perry cannot cook) with rice and a green salad, followed by an orgy of fresh fruit, with shortcake biscuits, and drank three bottles of Peregrine's excellent claret. (I am not a petty purist who refuses to drink wine with curry.) We then went on to coffee and whisky and Turkish delight. Thank God I have always had a good digestion. How sad for those who cannot enjoy what are after all prime pleasures of daily life, and perhaps for some the only ones, eating and drinking.

Iris Murdoch, The Sea, The Sea (1978).

'To dine in company'

One can say everything best over a meal.

George Eliot, Adam Bede (1859).

We cannot concoct our food with interruptions. Our chief meal, to be nutritive, must be solitary. With difficulty we can eat before a guest; and never understood what the relish of public feasting meant. Meats have no sapor, nor digestion fair play in a crowd.

Charles Lamb, 'That Home is No Home Though it is Never so
Homely' (1826).

To dine in company with more than two is a Gaulish and a German thing. I can hardly bring myself to believe that I have eaten in concert with twenty; so barbarous and herdlike a practice does it now appear to me: such an incentive to drink much and talk loosely; not to add, such a necessity to speak loud, which is clownish and odious in the extreme.

Walter Savage Landor, 'Lucellus and Caesar' (1829).

Dining-out is a vice, a dissipation of spirit punished by remorse. We eat, drink and talk a little too much, abuse all our friends, belch out our literary preferences and are egged on by accomplices in the audience to acts of mental exhibitionism. Such evenings cannot fail to diminish those who take part in them.

Cyril Connolly, *The Unquiet Grave* (1994).

It was a lesson in manners at lunch. Hubert and Eddie were particularly abandoned, cramming ham & gherkins into their mouths, slopping drink about, & behaving in a thoroughly aristocratic fashion. When Tim got up, Hubert spread mayonnaise on the bench, hoping he'd sit down in it, but Sandy, of course, who rather grandly partook only of a bread-roll & a glass of champagne, shouted out to him just in time, & earned some sullen gratitude. I ate, I think I can say, in a perfectly decorous fashion, with a slight sprawling over the table in deference to the occasion.

Alan Hollinghurst, *The Swimming-pool Library* (1988).

Society, my beloved Bob, has the eminent advantage over all other – that is, if there be any society left in the wretched distracted old European continent – that it is above all others a dinner-giving society. A people like the Germans, that dines habitually, and with what vast appetite I need not say, at one o'clock in the afternoon – like the Italians, that spends it evenings in opera-boxes – like the French, that amuses itself of nights with *eau sucrée* and intrigue – cannot, believe me, understand Society rightly. I love and admire my nation for its good sense, its manliness, its friendliness, its morality in the main – and these, I take it, are all expressed in that noble institution, the dinner.

The dinner is the happy end of the Briton's day. We work harder than the other nations of the earth. We do more, we live more in our time, than Frenchmen or Germans. Every great man amongst us likes his dinner, and takes to it kindly.

William Makepeace Thackeray, *The Book of Snobs* (1846).

Sunday supper, unless done on a large and informal scale, is probably the most depressing meal in existence. There is a chill discomfort in the round of beef, an icy severity about the open jam tart. The blancmange shivers miserably.

Spirituous liquor helps to counteract the influence of these things, and so does exhilarating conversation.

Unfortunately, at Mr Waller's table there was neither.

P.G. Wodehouse, *Psmith in the City* (1923).

She perceived that even personalities were failing to hold the party. The room filled with hesitancy as with a fog. People cleared their throats, tried to choke down yawns. The men shot their cuffs and the women stuck their combs more firmly into their back hair.

Then a rattle, a daring hope in every eye, the swinging of a door, the smell of strong coffee, Dave Dyer's mewing voice in a triumphant, 'The eats!' They began to chatter. They had something to do. They could escape from themselves. They fell upon the food – chicken sandwiches, maple cake, drug-store ice cream. Even when the food was gone they remained cheerful. They could go home, any time now, and go to bed!

Sinclair Lewis, *Main Street* (1920).

'The man who can carve'

Captain Forrester still made a commanding figure at the head of his own table, with his napkin tucked under this chin and the work of carving well in hand. Nobody could lay bare the bones of a brace of duck or a twenty-pound turkey more deftly. 'What part of the turkey do you prefer, Mrs Ogden?' If one had a preference, it was gratified, with all the stuffing and gravy that went with it, and the vegetables properly placed. When a plate left Captain Forrester's hands, it was a dinner; the recipient was served, and well served.

Willa Cather, *A Lost Lady* (1923).

At last the Red Queen began, 'You've missed the soup and fish,' she said. 'Put on the joint!' And the waiters set a leg of mutton before Alice, who looked at it rather anxiously, as she had never had to carve one before.

'You look a little shy; let me introduce you to that leg of mutton,' said the Red Queen. 'Alice – Mutton; Mutton – Alice.' The leg of mutton got up in the dish and made a little bow to Alice; and she returned the bow, not knowing whether to be frightened or amused.

'May I give you a slice?' she said, taking up the knife and fork, and looking from one Queen to the other.

'Certainly not,' the Red Queen said, very decidedly, 'it isn't etiquette to cut anyone you've been introduced to. Remove the joint!' And the waiters carried it off, and brought a large plum-pudding in its place.

'I won't be introduced to the pudding please,' Alice said rather hastily, 'or we shall get no dinner at all. May I give you some?'

But the Red Queen looked sulky, and growled, 'Pudding –
Alice; Alice – Pudding. Remove the pudding!' and the waiters
took it away before Alice could return its bow.

Lewis Carroll, *Through the Looking-Glass* (1872).

You have met *The Man Who Can Carve*? No matter if the
dish be a solitary roast pigeon, the coat is taken off, two square
yards of table cleared, several inoffensive diners compelled to
leave the room to give the ruffian 'a bit of freedom.' By some
miracle everything carved by this person is transformed into
scrag-ends, so that *nobody* gets anything that is eatable.

Flann O'Brien, *The Best of Myles* (1993).

Harvey probably knew how to carve a goose, but it was
his co-ordination that proved such a handicap. We all got
large pieces of hot, crisp, juicy, oily goose and we had a large
plate of those bread-rolls that come with great chunks of sea-
salt and poppy seeds baked to the top of them. There was
slivovice which Harvey liked and tiny pots of Turkish coffee
of which he wasn't so fond. We ate in greedy silence.

Len Deighton, *Funeral in Berlin* (1964).

In carving a partridge I splashed her with gravy from head
to foot; and though I saw three distinct brown rills of animal
juice trickling down her cheek, she had the complaisance to
swear that not a drop had reached her. Such circumstances
are the triumphs of civilised life.

Sydney Smith, quoted by Hesketh Pearson in *The Smith of Smiths*
(1875).

My particular memory is of a quail-pie. Quails may be
alright for Moses in the desert, but, if they are served in the
form of a pie at dinner, they should be distributed at a side-
table, not handed round from guest to guest. The Countess

having shuddered at it and resumed her biscuit, it was left to me to make the opening excavation. The difficulty was to know where each quail began and ended; the job really wanted a professional quail-finder, who might have indicated the point on the surface of the crust at which it would be most helpful to dig for quails.

As it was, I had to dig at random, and, being unlucky, I plunged the knife straight into the middle of a bird. It was impossible, of course, to withdraw the quail through the slit I had thus made in the pastry, nor could I get my knife out (with a bird sticking on the end of it) in order to make a second slit at a suitable angle. I tried to shake the quail off inside the pie, but it was fixed too firmly. I tried pulling it off against the inside of the crust, but it became obvious that if I persisted in this, the whole roof would come off. The footman, with great presence of mind, realized my difficulty and offered me a second knife. Unfortunately, I misjudged the width of the quails and plunging the second knife into the pie a little further on, I landed into the middle of another quail no less retentive of cutlery than the first. The dish now began to look more like a game than a pie, and, waving away a third knife, I said (quite truly by this time) that I didn't like quails and on second thought I would ask the Dowager Countess to lend me a biscuit.

A.A. Milne, 'Going Out to Dinner' (1920).

'There was an abundance of food'

They made supper ready and, on top of the usual fare there were roasted sixteen oxen, three heifers, thirty-two calves, sixty-three suckling kids, ninety-five sheep, three hundred suckling pigs in wine sauce, eleven score partridges, seven hundred woodcock, four hundred capons from Loudon and Cornouaille, six thousand pullets and as many pigeons, six hundred guinea-fowl, fourteen hundred leverets, three hundred and three bustards, and one thousand and seven hundred capon chicks.

Game they could not get so quickly, except eleven wild boars sent by the abbot of Turpenay, and eighteen fallow deer presented by the Lord of Grandmont, together with seven score pheasants sent by the Lord of Essars and some dozen of ring-doves, water-hens, teal, bitterns, curlews, plovers, heathcock, briganders, sea ducks, young lapwings, sheldrakes, shovelers, herons, hernshaws, coots, criels, storks, little bustards orange flamingos (which are called *phoenicopters*), landrails, and turkey hens, together with plenty of dumplings and quantities of soups.

There was an abundance of food there, and no mistake.

François Rabelais, *Gargantua* (1534).

I never saw any thing equal to the comfort and style – Candles everywhere – I was telling you of your grandmama, Jane, – There was a little disappointment – The baked apples and biscuits, excellent in their way, you know; but there was a delicate fricassee of sweetbread and some asparagus brought in at first, and good Mr Woodhouse, not thinking the asparagus quite boiled enough, sent it all out again. Now there is nothing grandmama loves better than sweetbread and asparagus – so she was rather disappointed, but we agreed we would not speak of it to anybody, for fear of its getting round to dear Miss Woodhouse, who would be so very much concerned! – Well, this is brilliant! I am all amazement! could not have supposed any thing! – Such elegance and profusion! – I have seen nothing like it since – Well where shall we sit? where shall we sit? Any where, so that Jane is not in a draught. Where *I* sit is of no consequence. Oh! Do you recommend this side? – Well I am sure, Mr Churchill – only it seems too good – but just as you please. What you direct in this house cannot be wrong. Dear Jane, how shall we ever recollect half the dishes for grandmama? Soup too! Bless me! I should not be helped so soon, but it smells most excellent, and I cannot help beginning.

Jane Austen, *Emma* (1815).

The lunch on this occasion began with soles, sunk in a deep dish, over which the college cook had spread a counter-pane of the whitest cream, save that it was branded here and there with brown spots like the spots on the flanks of a doe. After that came the partridges, but if this suggests a couple of bald, brown birds on a plate you are mistaken. The partridges, many and various, came with all their retinue of sauces and salads, the sharp and the sweet, each in its order, their potatoes, thin as coins but not so hard; their sprouts, foliated as rosebuds but more succulent. And no sooner had the roast and its retinue been done with than the silent serving-man, the Beadle himself perhaps in a milder manifestation, set before us, wreathed in napkins, a confection which rose all sugar from the waves. To call it pudding and so relate it to rice and tapioca would be an insult.

Virginia Woolf, *A Room of One's Own* (1928).

It was a magnificent spread, and of inordinate length. Dish followed dish; golden cider and red wine fraternized in neighbouring glasses, to mingle later inside. The clatter of plates, the hum of conversation and the soft music of the band combined to make a continuous low murmur, which faded into the silence of the cloudless sky among the darting swallows. From time to time Mme. Husson straightened her black silk wig, which somehow got tilted rakishly over one ear, as she chatted with Father Malou. The Mayor was talking politics passionately with Major Desbarres, and Isidore went on eating and drinking all the time, as he had never eaten and drunk before. He took a helping, often two, of everything, realizing for the first time how comforting it is to feel one's belly filling up with good things, which one has first savoured on the tongue. He had skilfully undone the top button of his trousers, which were getting uncomfortable tight under the increasing pressure of this stomach: he did not talk much, and, though he was a little worried over the stain of a drop of wine that had fallen on his duck coat, he stopped eating at frequent intervals to raise his glass to his lips, drinking as slowly as possible in order to prolong the enjoyment.

Guy de Maupassant, 'Madam Husson's May King' (1888).

'Loaded with good cheer'

Then Bacchus and Silenus and the Maenads began a dance, far wilder than the dance of the trees; not merely a dance for fun and beauty (though it was that too) but a dance of plenty, and where their hands touched, and where their feet fell, the feast came into existence – sides of roasted meat that filled the grove with delicious smell, and wheaten cakes and oaten cakes, honey and many coloured sugars and cream as thick as porridge and as smooth as still water, peaches, nectarines, pomegranates, pears, grapes, strawberries, raspberries – pyramids and cataracts of fruit. Then, in great wooden cups and bowls and mazers, wreathed with ivy, came the wines; dark, thick ones like syrups of mulberry juice, and clear red ones like jellies liquefied, and yellow wines and green wines and yellow-green and greenish-yellow.

C.S. Lewis, *Prince Caspian* (1951).

There was never such a Christmas dinner as they had that day. The fat turkey was a sight to behold, when Hannah sent him up, stuffed, browned, and decorated. So was the plum pudding, which melted in one's mouth, likewise the jellies, in which Amy revelled like a fly in a honeypot. Everything turned out well, which was a mercy. Hannah said, 'For my mind was that flustered, Mum, that it's a merrycle that I didn't roast the pudding and stuff the turkey with raisins, let alone bilin' of it in a cloth.'

Louisa M. Alcott, *Little Women* (1868).

The table was literally loaded with good cheer, and presented an epitome of country abundance, in this season of overflowing larders. A distinguished post was allotted to 'ancient sirloin,' as mine host termed it; being, as he added, 'the standard of old English hospitality, and a joint of goodly presence, and full of expectation.' There were several dishes quaintly decorated, and which had evidently something traditional in their embellishments; but about which, as I did not like to appear over-curious, I asked no questions.

I could not, however, but notice a pie, magnificently decorated with peacock's feathers, in imitation of the tail of that bird, which overshadowed a considerable tract of the table. This, the squire confessed, with some little hesitation, was a pheasant pie, though a peacock pie was certainly the most authentical; but there had been such a mortality among the peacocks this season, that he could not prevail upon himself to have one killed.

Washington Irving, 'The Christmas Dinner' (1819).

As to the dinner, it's perfectly delightful – nothing goes wrong, and everybody is in the very best of spirits, and disposed to please and be pleased. Grandpapa relates a circumstantial account of the purchase of previous turkeys, on former

Christmas-days, which grandmamma corroborates in the minutest particular. Uncle George tells stories, and carves poultry, and takes wine, and jokes with the children at the side-table, and winks at the cousins that are making love, or being made love to, and exhilarates everybody with this good humour and hospitality; and when, at last a stout servant staggers in with a gigantic pudding, with a sprig of holly in the top, there is such a laughing, and shouting, and clapping of little chubby hands, and kicking up of fat dumpy legs, as can only be equalled by the applause with which the astonishing feat of pouring lighted brandy into mince-pies is received by the younger visitors. Then the dessert! – and the wine! – and the fun!

Charles Dickens, 'A Christmas Dinner' (1836).

It was the usual Australian Christmas dinner, taking place in the middle of the day. Despite the temperature being 1000 F. in the shade, there had been the full panoply of raging hot food, topped off with a volcanic plum pudding smothered in scalding custard. My mother had naturally spiced the pudding with sixpences and threepenny bits, called zacs and trays respectively. Grandpa had collected one of these in the oesophagus. He gave a protracted, strangled gurgle which for a long time we all took to be the beginning of some anecdote. Then Aunt Dot bounded out of her chair and hit him in the back. By some miracle she did not snap his calcified spine. Coated with black crumbs and custard, the zac streaked out of his mouth like a dum-dum and ricocheted off a tureen.

Clive James, *Unreliable Memoirs* (1980).

Athelny laughed boisterously. Sally brought them plates of rice pudding, rich, creamy, and luscious. Athelny attacked his with gusto.

'One of the rules of this house is that Sunday dinner should never alter. It is a ritual. Roast beef and rice pudding for fifty

Sundays in the year. On Easter Sunday lamb and green peas, and at Michaelmas roast goose and apple sauce. Thus we preserve the traditions of our people. When Sally marries she will forget many of the wise things I have taught her, but she will never forget that if you want to be good and happy you must eat on Sundays roast beef and rice pudding.'

'You'll call when you're ready for cheese,' said Sally impassively.

W. Somerset Maugham, *Of Human Bondage* (1915).

The wedding-feast had been laid in the cart-shed. On the table were four sirloins, six dishes of hashed chicken, some stewed veal, three legs of mutton, and in the middle a nice roast sucking-pig flanked by four sausages with sorrel. Flasks of brandy stood at the corners. A rich foam had frothed out round the corks of the cider-bottles. Every glass had already been filled to the brim with wine. Yellow custard stood in big dishes, shaking at the slightest jog of the table, with the initials of the newly wedded couple traced on its smooth surface in arabesques of sugared almond. For the tarts and confectioneries they had hired a pastry-cook from Yvetot. He was new to the district, and so had taken great pains with his work. At dessert he brought in with his own hands a tiered cake that made them all cry out. It started off at the base with a square of blue cardboard representing a temple with porticoes and colonnades, with stucco statuettes all round it in recesses studded with gilt-paper stars; on the second layer was a castle-keep in Savoy cake, surrounded by tiny fortifications in angelica, almonds, raisins and quarters of orange; and finally, on the uppermost platform, which was a green meadow with rocks, pools of ham and boats of nutshell, stood a little Cupid, poised on a chocolate swing whose uprights had two real rose-buds for knobs at the top.

Gustave Flaubert, *Madame Bovary* (1857).

6. MOOD

'Eating is the only thing that consoles me'

My mum, I missed her so much. I didn't wash my clothes because I could still smell the faintest fragrance of her cooking on them. I'd sit there, on the floor by the manky old wall heater, a shirt or jumper in my hands, recalling the array of her specialities: keema, gosht, saag cholay, puree, halwa, chaat, stuffed kerala, lassi saag, and on the mental list went, with me reliving and salivating over the mere thought of any one of her meals, thinking about the care she took over them, the pleasure I took in eating them. Even something simple like roti she prayed over as she slapped off the excess flour, both hands working as one, stretching, spreading and caressing the dough into a perfect circle every time.

M.Y. Alam, *Kilo* (2002).

'Now, cheer up, Toad,' she said coaxingly, on entering, 'and sit up and dry your eyes and be a sensible animal. And do try and eat a bit of dinner. See, I've brought you some of mine, hot from the oven!'

It was bubble-and-squeak, between two plates, and its fragrance filled the narrow cell. The penetrating smell of cabbage reached the nose of Toad as he lay prostrate in his misery on the floor, and gave him the idea for a moment that perhaps life was not such a blank and desperate thing as he had imagined. But still he wailed, and kicked with his legs, and refused to be comforted. So the wise girl retired for the time, but, of course, a good deal of the smell of hot cabbage remained behind, as it will do, and Toad, between his sobs, sniffed and reflected, and gradually began to think new and inspiring thoughts: of chivalry, and poetry, and deeds still to be done; of broad meadows, and cattle browsing in them, raked by sun and wind; of kitchen-gardens, and straight herb-boarders, and warm snap-dragon beset by bees; and of the comforting clink of dishes set down on the table at Toad Hall, and the scrape of chair-legs on the floor as everyone pulled himself close up to this work.

Kenneth Grahame, *The Wind in the Willows* (1908).

JACK: How can you sit there, calmly eating muffins when we are in this horrible trouble, I can't make out. You seem to me to be perfectly heartless.

ALGERNON: Well, I can't eat muffins in an agitated manner. The butter would probably get on my cuffs. One should always eat muffins quite calmly. It is the only way to eat them.

JACK: I say it's perfectly heartless your eating muffins at all, under the circumstances.

ALGERNON: When I am in trouble, eating is the only thing that consoles me. Indeed, when I am in really great trouble, as anyone who knows me intimately will tell you, I refuse everything except food and drink. At the present moment I am eating muffins because I am unhappy. Besides, I am particularly fond of muffins.

Oscar Wilde, *The Importance of Being Earnest* (1895).

The cheering sound of 'Dinner is upon the table,' dissolved his reverie, and we *all* sat down without any symptom of ill humour. There were present, besides Mr Wilkes, and Mr Arthur Lee, who was an old companion of mine when he studied physick at Edinburgh, Mr (now Sir

John) Miller, Dr Lettsom, and Mr Slater the druggist. Mr Wilkes placed himself next to Dr Johnson, and behaved to him with so much attention and politeness, that he gained upon him insensibly. No man eats more heartily than Johnson, or loved better what was nice and delicate. Mr Wilkes was very assiduous in helping him to some fine veal. 'Pray give me leave, Sir: – It is better here – A little of the brown – Some fat, Sir – A little of the stuffing – Some of the gravy – Let me have the pleasure of giving you some butter – Allow me to recommend a squeeze of this orange; – or the lemon, perhaps, may have more zest.' – 'Sir, sir, I am obliged to you, Sir,' cried Johnson, bowing, and turning his head to him with a look for some time of 'surly virtue,' but, in a short while, of complacency.

James Boswell, *Life of Johnson* (1791).

Tho' Gluttonizing, if I may use that Expression, is what I am an utter Enemy to, yet moderate Eating I have often observed was conducive to Good Humour, and had no surprising Effect on the Tempers of Mankind. A Lady of my Acquaintance, is, as soon as she is out of Bed, as ill-natur'd a Woman as any in Great Britain; she is peevish with every Body about her, she is angry at she don't know what, and scolds she don't know why; but from the Moment she has swallow'd her first Dish of Tea and eat her first Piece of Bread and Butter, she begins to smile, her Frowardness imperceptibly vanishes and her Hunger decreases, and then continues the kindest Mistress, the tenderest Mother, and the quietest Wife in the three Kingdoms 'till she wants to eat again.

'Gluttony', *The Universal Spectator* (1736).

'Sensuality was circulating in the house'

Directly the victuals are discussed, and John takes away the plate, my tongue begins to wag. Does not yours, if you have a pleasant neighbour? – a lovely creature, say, of some five-and-thirty, whose daughters have not yet come out – they are the best talkers.

William Makepeace Thackeray, *The Book of Snobs* (1846).

Now, the most pleasant feature of lunch at a country house is this – that you may sit next to whomsoever you please. At dinner she may be entrusted to quite the wrong man; at breakfast you are faced with the problem of being neither too early for her nor yet too late for a seat beside her; at tea people have a habit of taking your chair at the moment when a simple act of courtesy has drawn you from it in search of bread and butter; but at lunch you follow her in and there you are – fixed.

A.A. Milne, 'Lunch' (1934).

There is no more charming sight than a pretty gourmand in action: her napkin is daintily tucked in; one hand rests on the table; the other conveys to her mouth elegantly cut morsels, or the wing of a partridge for her teeth to bite; her eyes are bright, her lips glistening, and all her movements full of grace; and she does not lack that touch of coquetry which women show in everything they do. With such advantages she is irresistible, and even Cato the Censor could not look at her unmoved.

Jean-Anthelme Brillat-Savarin, *Physiologie du Goût* (1825).

Angelica, the lovely Angelica, forgot little Tuscan black-puddings and part of her good manners and devoured her food with the appetite of her seventeen years and the vigour given by grasping her fork half-way up the handle. Tancredi, in an attempt to link gallantry with greed, tried to imagine himself tasting, in the aromatic forkfuls, the kisses of his neighbour Angelica, but he realised at once that the experiment was disgusting and suspended it, with a mental reserve about reviving this fantasy with the pudding; the Prince, although rapt in the contemplation of Angelica sitting opposite him, was the only one at table able to notice that the demi-glace was overfilled, and made a mental note to tell the cook so next day; the others ate without thinking of anything, and without realising that the food seemed so delicious because sensuality was circulating in the house.

Giuseppe di Lampedusa, *The Leopard* (1958).

He conducted her about the lawns, and flower-beds, and conservatories; and thence to the fruit-garden and green-houses, where he asked her if she liked strawberries.

'Yes,' said Tess, 'when they come.'

'They are already here.' D'Urberville began gathering specimens of the fruit for her, handing them back to her as he stooped; and, presently, selecting a specially fine product of the 'British Queen' variety, he stood up and held it by the stem to her mouth.

'No – no!' she said quickly, putting her fingers between and him and her lips. 'I would rather take it in my own hand.'

'Nonsense!' he insisted; and in a slight distress she parted her lips and took it in.

Thomas Hardy, *Tess of the D'Urbervilles* (1891).

The servant took away the empty dishes and came back with an earthenware bowl of crayfish swimming in a steaming, delicious-smelling, spicy broth. They devoured them with great gusto. Joyce added even more pepper and then stuck out her tongue as if it were on fire. Alec slowly poured the chilled wine; it made the glasses turn misty.

'We'll have champagne in our room tonight, as we always do,' murmured Joyce, slightly tipsy, while cracking an enormous crayfish between her teeth. 'What kind of champagne do they have? I want some Cliquot, very dry.'

She raised her glass between her cupped hands.

'Look . . . the wine is the same colour as the moon tonight, all golden . . .'

They drank together from the same glass, merging their moist, peppery lips, lips so young that nothing could change the way they tasted of ripe fruit.

With the chicken sautéed with olives and sweet pimentos, they drank a bottle of ruby Chambertin, full-bodied and warm, that left a wonderful taste in the mouth. Then Alec ordered some brandy and poured drops of it into two large glasses of champagne. Joyce drank.

Irène Némirovsky, *David Golder* (1929).

Together they pulled everything out of the refrigerator, and produced a feast of Jewish salami and feta cheese and hard-boiled eggs and tomatoes and black bread and sweet butter and half-sour pickles and big black Greek olives and raw Spanish onions and beer, and trotted all of it back to bed with them and sat there gorging themselves and talking and drinking and laughing and touching each other.

Marilyn French, *The Women's Room* (1978).

She was so much transported with her good fortune, that she could not contain her exstasy, but flew upon me like a tygeress, and pressed her skinny lips to mine; when (as it was no doubt concerted by her evil genius) a dose of garlick she had swallowed that morning, to dispel wind I suppose, began to operate with such a sudden explosion, that human nature, circumstanced as I was, could not endure the shock with any degree of temper. – I lost all patience and reflection, flung away from her in an instant, snatched my hat and cane, and run down stairs as the devil had me in pursuit and could scarce restrain the convulsion of my bowels, which were grievously offended by the perfume that assaulted me.

Tobias Smollett, The Adventures of Roderick Random (1748).

I am sometimes stupid enough to eat a lot of hot things with the purpose of testing whether my reproductive powers have been destroyed or not; I did this yesterday and so I had diarrhoea and was upset all day. *I must try to arouse sensuality as little as possible.*

Leo Tolstoy, diary entry, 30 March, 1852.

'An adjunct to a refined gluttony'

Give me Books, fruit, French wine and fine weather and a little music out of doors, played by somebody I do not know.

John Keats, letter to Fanny Keats, 28th August 1819.

'My idea of heaven is, eating *pâtés de fois gras* to the sound of trumpets.'

Sidney Smith, quoted by H. Pearson in The Smith of Smiths (1934).

As to the dinner itself – the mere dinner – it goes off much the same every where. Tureens of soup are emptied with awful rapidity – waiters take plates of turbot away, to get lobster-sauce, and bring back plates of lobster-sauce, without turbot; people who can carve poultry, are great fools if they own it, and people who can't, have no wish to learn. – The knives and forks form a pleasing accompaniment to Auber's music, and Auber's music would form a pleasing accompaniment to the dinner, if you could hear any thing besides the cymbals.

Charles Dickens, 'Public Dinners' (1836).

It seems to me an intolerable insult to a musical artist that people should treat his art as an adjunct to a refined gluttony. It seems a yet more subtle insult to the musician that people should require to be fortified with food and drink at intervals, to strengthen them to endure his music. I say nothing of the deeper and darker insult to that other artist, the cook, in suggestion that men require to be inspired and rallied with drums and trumpets to attack the dangers of his dinner, as if it were a fortress bristling with engines of death. But in any case it is the combination of the two pleasures that is unpleasant. When people are listening to a good concert they do not ostentatiously produce large pork-pies and bottles of beer to enable them to get through it somehow. And if they do not bring their meals to their music, why should they bring their music to their meals?

G. K. Chesterton, 'On Pleasure-seeking' (1939).

It was a gala evening at the Grand Sybaris Hotel, and a special dinner was being served in the Amethyst dining-hall. The Amethyst dining-hall had almost a European reputation, especially with that section of Europe which is historically identified with the Jordan Valley. Its cooking was beyond reproach, and its orchestra was sufficiently highly salaried to be above criticism. Thither came in shoals, the intensely musical and the almost intensely musical, who are very many, and in still greater numbers the merely musical, who know how Tschaikowsky's name is pronounced and can recognize several of Chopin's nocturnes if you give them due warning; these eat in the nervous, detached manner of roebuck feeding in the open, and keep anxious ears cocked towards the orchestra for the first hint of a recognizable melody.

'Ah, yes, *Pagliacci*,' they murmur, as the opening strains follow hot upon the soup, and if no contradiction is forthcoming from any better-informed quarter they break forth into subdued humming by way of supplementing the efforts of the musicians. Sometimes the melody starts on level terms with the soup, in which case the banqueters contrive somehow to hum between the spoonfuls; the facial expression of enthusiasts who are punctuating potage St Germain with Pagliacci is not beautiful, but it should be seen by those who are bent on observing all sides of life. One cannot discount the unpleasant things of this world merely by looking the other way.

In addition to the aforementioned types the restaurant was patronized by a fair sprinkling of the absolutely non-musical; their presence in the dining-hall could only be explained on the supposition that they had come there to dine.

The earlier stages of the dinner had worn off. The wine lists had been consulted, by some with the blank embarrassment of a schoolboy suddenly called on to locate a Minor Prophet in the tangled hinterland of the Old Testament, by others with the severe scrutiny which suggests that they have visited most of the higher-priced wines in their own homes and probed their family weaknesses. The diners who chose their wine in the latter fashion always gave their orders in a penetrating voice, with a plentiful garnishing of stage direction. By insisting on having your bottle pointing to the north when the cork is being drawn, or calling the waiter Max, you may induce an impression on your guests which hours of laboured boasting might be powerless to achieve. For this purpose, however, the guests must be chosen as carefully as the wine.

Standing aside from the revellers in the shadow of a massive pillar was an interested spectator who was assuredly of the feast, and yet not in it. Monsieur Aristide Saucourt was the chef of the Grand Sybaris Hotel, and if he had an equal in his profession he had never acknowledged the fact. In his own domain he was a potentate, hedged around with the cold brutality the Genius expects rather than excuses in her children; he never forgave, and those who served him were careful that there should be little to forgive. In the outer world, the world which devoured his creations, he was an influence; how profound or how shallow an influence he never attempted to guess. It is the penalty and the safeguard of genius that it computes itself by troy weight in a world that measures by vulgar hundredweights.

Once in a way the great man would be seized with a desire to watch the effects of his master-efforts, just as the guiding brain of Krupp's might wish at a supreme moment to intrude into the firing line of an artillery duel. And such an occasion was the present. For the first time in the history of the Grand Sybaris Hotel, he was presenting to its guests the dish which he had brought to that pitch of perfection which almost amounts to scandal. Canetons à la mode d'Amblève. In thin gilt lettering on the creamy white of the menu how little those words conveyed to the bulk of the imperfectly educated diners. And yet how much specialized effort had been lavished, and how much carefully treasured lore had been ungarnered, before those six words could be written. In the Department of Deux-Sèvres ducklings had lived peculiar and beautiful lives and died in the odour of satiety to furnish the main theme of the dish; champignons, which even a purist for Saxon English would have hesitated to address as mushrooms, had contributed their languorous atrophied bodies to the garnishing, and a sauce devised in the twilight reign of the Fifteenth Louis had been summoned back from the imperishable past to take its part in the wonderful confection. Thus far had human effort laboured to achieve the desired result; the rest had been left to human genius – the genius of Aristide Saucourt.

And now the moment had arrived for the serving of the great dish, the dish which world-weary Grand Dukes and market-obsessed money magnates counted among their happiest memories. And at the same moment something else happened. The leader of the highly salaried orchestra placed his violin caressingly against his chin, lowered his eyelids, and floated into a sea of melody.

'Hark!' said most of the diners, 'he is playing "The Chaplet".'

They knew it was 'The Chaplet' because they had heard it played at luncheon and afternoon tea, and at supper the night before, and had not had time to forget.

'Yes, he is playing "The Chaplet", they reassured one another. The general voice was unanimous on the subject. The orchestra had already played it eleven times that day, four times by desire and seven times from force of habit, but the familiar strains were greeted with the rapture due to a revelation. A murmur of much humming rose from half the tables in the room, and some of the more over-wrought listeners laid down knife and fork in order to be able to burst in with loud clappings at the earliest permissible moment.

And the Canetons à la mode d'Amblève? In stupefied, sickening wonder Aristide watched them grow cold in total neglect, or suffer the almost worse indignity of perfunctory pecking and listless munching while the banqueters lavished their approval and applause on the music-makers. Calves' livers and bacon, with parsley sauce, could hardly have figured more ignominiously in the evening's entertainment. And while the master of culinary art leaned back against the sheltering pillar, choking with a horrible brain-searing rage that could find no outlet for its agony, the orchestra leader was bowing his acknowledgments of the hand-clappings that rose in a storm around him. Turning to his colleagues he nodded the signal for an encore. But before the violin had been lifted anew into position there came from the shadow of the pillar an explosive negative.

'Noh! Noh! You do not play thot again!'

The musician turned in furious astonishment. Had he taken warning from the look in the other man's eyes he might have acted differently. But the admiring plaudits were ringing in his ears, and he snarled out sharply, 'That is for me to decide.'

'Noh! You play thot never again,' shouted the chef, and the next moment he had flung himself violently upon the loathed being who had supplanted him in the world's esteem. A large metal tureen, filled to the brim with steaming soup, had just been placed on a side table in readiness for a late party of diners; before the waiting staff or the guests had time to realize what was happening, Aristide had dragged his struggling victim up to the table and plunged his head deep down into the almost boiling contents on the tureen. At the further end of the room the diners were still spasmodically applauding in view of an encore.

Whether the leader of the orchestra died from drowning by soup, or from the shock to his professional vanity, or was scalded to death, the doctors were never wholly able to agree. Monsieur Aristide Saucourt, who now lives in complete retirement, always inclined to the drowning theory.

H.H. Munro (Saki), 'The Chaplet' (1911).

7. EATING ESTABLISHMENTS

'Don't talk to me about taverns!'

A beefsteak-house is a most excellent place to dine at. You come there to a warm, comfortable, large room, where a number of people are sitting at table. You take whatever place you find empty; call for what you like, which you get well and cleverly dressed. You may either chat or not as you like. Nobody minds you, and you pay very reasonably. My dinner (beef, bread and beer and water) was only a shilling.

James Boswell, journal entry, 15 December, 1762.

Before I leave this inn I will add that for lunch they gave us soup, Yorkshire pudding, roast chicken and sausages and two vegetables, fruit pudding, cheese and biscuits, and coffee, all for two and sixpence each. And that – when they have a mind to – is the way they do it in Yorkshire.

J. B. Priestley, *English Journey* (1934).

The most famous hot-buttered toast house in the world was 'Tyson's Restaurant' in Rook Street, Manchester, which still flourishes, but is no longer animated by the crisp individuality of its founder, old Tom Tyson, as he was known. Tyson, a born autocrat, knew that in their heart of hearts Britons, for all their Rule-Britannia sentiments, like to be slave-driven. So he established a restaurant wherein he, an inflexible tyrant, might enforce laws of his own making and win riches by this very enforcement. He provided only chops, steaks, and Cumberland ham, and served with them, instead of vegetables, hot buttered toast or bread. Most of his customers took toast. People who asked for potatoes were unceremoniously told that they should have brought their own. Everyone who ate at Tyson's was compelled also to drink. Ale, stout, coffee, and tea were the only liquids. A customer asking for water was referred to the 'teetotal shop next door.'

A host of good stories are told of Tyson. He dominated the place in his shirt-sleeves, and nothing escaped his vigilant eye. His duty to a customer, as he conceived it, was done when good food had been laid promptly before him; after that the customer's duty to the master of the restaurant began. Reading was not permitted, at least in the middle of the day, nor grumbling, nor a protracted sitting, nor smoking. Tyson's strength was in the excellence of his wares, his cheapness, and his business-like dispatch, and knowing this he played the Kaiser to the top of his bent. A young man once calling, 'Waiter, bring me a steak at once,' was amazed to find a raw steak clapped on the table before him. To his expression of disgust came the reply, 'You can't expect meat to be cooked if you want it at once.' Another customer had the temerity to complain that the steak was tough. A considerable space of time elapsed before he came again, but Tyson, who forgot nothing, was waiting for him. The grumbler called for steak. 'Steaks are tough,' was the reply. 'Then I'll have a chop.' 'Chops are tough.' 'Then what can I have?' 'Nothing. If you can't be satisfied with food that pleases other people you can go somewhere else.' A customer daring so much as to glance at a letter from his pocket was curtly informed that 'this is not a library.' A customer who had exceeded his welcome was bidden to go. To the few who complained of his incivility, Tyson's reply was that he served his civility with his chops and steaks.

E.V. Lucas, 'A Word on Toast' (1906).

Don't talk to me about taverns! There is just one genuine, clean, decent, palatable thing occasionally to be had in them – namely, a boiled egg. The soups taste pretty good sometimes, but their sources are involved in a darker mystery than that of the Nile. Omelettes taste as if they had been carried in the waiter's hat, or fried in an old boot. I ordered scrambled eggs one day. It must be that they had been scrambled for by somebody, but who – who in the possession of a sound reason could have scrambled for what I had set before me under that name? Butter! I am thinking just now of those exquisite little pellets I have so often seen at your table, and wondering why the taverns always keep it until it is old. Fool that I am! As if the taverns did not know that if it was good it would be eaten, which is not what they want. Then the waiters with the napkins – what don't they do with those napkins! Mention any one thing of which you think you can say with truth 'That they do not do'.

Oliver Wendell Holmes, 'Life and Letters' (1867).

The typical Bowery eating house is a long-high-ceilinged room with a plate-glass storewindow in front for all its light by day. There are long wooden tables varnished with gravy, which has been massaged into the grain of the wood in the course of years. Salt and pepper are in open dishes and the customers reach in with their hands. The average check is ten cents, and payment entitles the customer to sit up all night and keep out of the cold.

A.J. Liebling, *Back Where I Came From* (1938).

I followed his example in the middle of cook's shop, almost suffocated with the steams of boil'd beef, and surrounded by a company consisting chiefly of hackney-coachmen, chairmen, draymen, and a few footmen out of place or on board wages; who sat eating shin of beef, tripe, cow-heel or sausages, at separate boards, covered with cloths, which turned my stomach. – While I stood in amaze, undetermined whether to sit down or walk upwards again, Strap, in his descent missing one of the steps, tumbled headlong into this infernal ordinary, and overturned the cook as she was carrying the porringer of soup to one of the guests: In her fall, she dashed the whole mess against the legs of a drummer belonging to the foot guards, who happened to be in her way, and scalded him so miserably, that he started up, and danced up and down, uttering a volley of execrations that made my hair stand on end. While he entertained the company in this manner, with an eloquence peculiar to himself, the cook got up, and after a hearty curse on the poor author of this mischance, who lay under the table scratching his rump with a woful countenance, emptied a salt-seller in her hand, and stripping down the patient's stocking which brought the skin along with it, applied the contents to the sore.

Tobias Smollett, *The Adventures of Roderick Random* (1748).

Fishiest of all fishy places was the Try Pots, which well deserved its name; for the pots there were always boiling chowders. Chowder for breakfast, and chowder for dinner, and chowder for supper, till you began to look for fish-bones coming through your clothes. The area before the house was paved with clam-shells. Mrs Hussey wore a polished necklace of codfish vertebra; and Hosea Hussey had his account books bound in superior old shark-skin. There was a fishy flavour to the milk, too, which I could not at all account for, till one morning happened to take a stroll along the beach among some fishermen's boats, I saw Hosea's brindled cow feeding on fish remnants, and marching along the sand with each foot in a cod's decapitated head, looking very slip-shot, I assure ye.

Herman Melville, *Moby Dick* (1851).

We joined a swelling stream of the citizens of Swindon, all following a series of notices marked 'British Restaurant', to a huge elephant-house, where thousands and thousands of human beings were eating as we did an enormous all-beige meal, starting with beige soup thickened to the consistency of paste, followed by beige mince full of lumps and garnished with beige beans and a few beige potatoes, then beige apple stew and a sort of skilly. Very satisfying and crushing, and calling up a vision of our future Planned World – all beige also.

Frances Partridge, *A Pacifist's War* (1978).

There was an almighty crowd coming out, pouring out of the place, still going Olé olé olé olé. It was mostly the younger ones. There was suddenly a couple of hundred people in the carpark, and then one of them saw the van.

Yeow!!

They stopped Oléing and looked at the van.

Charge!

Oh my fuck –, said Jimmy Sr. – Red alert; red alert. It was like Pearl fuckin' Harbor. Jimmy Sr had half said – Form a queue there, when they hit the van.

Oh, mother o'shite!

It hopped; they lifted it up off the road. One of the bars holding up the hatch skipped and Jimmy Sr just caught it before it fell and skulled someone outside.

A cod and large!

Curry chips, Mister.

Howyeh, Sharon!

OLÉ – OLÉ OLÉ OLÉ!

I was first!

Are yis Irish or Italians or wha'?

Yeow, Sharon!

Sharon; here! We're first, righ'.

Give us a C!!

Bimbo was covered in batter. Sharon was trying to get the spilt fat off her shoes.

Give us a H!!

It was madness out there; pande-fuckin'-monium.

Give us a I!!

There was a young one being crushed against the van. Her neck was digging into the counter.

Bimbo joined Jimmy Sr at the hatch.

Back now! he roared. – Push back there! There's people bein' crushed up here!

Fuck them!

Jimmy Sr pointed at the young fellow who'd said that.

You're barred!

They cheered, but they quietened down after that.

Give us a P!

The young one was rubbing her neck but she was alright. Jimmy Sr served her first.

What do you want?

Give us an S!

Jimmy Sr looked out over the crowd.

Will somebody shut tha' fuckin' eejit up! He roared.

Yeow!

They cheered and clapped, and Jimmy Sr started to enjoy himself. He lifted his arms and acknowledged the applause – Thank you, thank you – and then he got back to business.

Wha' was that? He asked the young one.

Curry chips, she said, raising her eyes to heaven.

No curry chips, Jimmy Sr told her.

Why not?

Cos we're not fuckin' Chinese, said Jimmy Sr. – This is an Irish Chipper.

That's stupih, said the young one.

Next!

Hang on, hang on! A large single an' – an' –

Hurry –

A spice-burger.

A large an' a spice, Sharon please!! Jimmy Sr roared over his shoulder. – Next. – You with the haircut there; wha' d'yeh want?

World peace.

You're barred. Next!

Roddy Doyle, The Van (1991).

'A dull, good, nice restaurant'

We dined at the Boeuf à la Mode. A dull, good, nice restaurant. I gave the waiter my usual 10%, which happened to be 70 centimes. He was apparently not content, but politely thanked me. As he carried the plate out with the change on it, he held it the least bit in the world at arm's length, exposing it with scorn to the inspection of the *chasseur* as he passed him. It was a fine, subtle gesture, and pleased me as much as it annoyed me.

Arnold Bennett, diary entry, 1 October, 1909.

'This way, please, your excellency. Your excellency won't be disturbed here,' said a particularly attentive, white-headed old Tartar, so broad across the hips that his coat-tails gaped behind. 'If you please, your hat, your excellency,' he said to Levin; by way of showing his respect of Oblonsky fussing round his guest as well.

In a twinkling, he flung a new cloth over the round table under a bronze chandelier, though it already had a table-cloth on it, pushed up velvet chairs, and came and stood before Oblonsky with a napkin and bill of fare in his hands, awaiting his order.

'If your excellency would prefer a private room, one will be available in a few moments – Prince Golizin is there with a lady. Fresh oysters are in.'

'Ah, oysters!'

Oblonsky considered.

'How about changing our menu, Levin?' he said, keeping his finger on the bill of fare, his face expressing serious hesitation. 'Are the oysters good? Be sure now!'

'They're Flensburg, your excellency: we've no Ostend.'

'Flensburg or not – are they fresh?'

'They only arrived yesterday, sir.'

'Well then, shall we start with oysters and change the whole programme? What do you think?'

'I don't mind. I like cabbage-soup and *kasha* better than anything; but I don't suppose they have that here.'

'*Kasha à la russe* your excellency would like?' said the Tartar, bending over Levin like a nurse over a child.

'No, seriously though, whatever you choose will suit me. Skating has given me an appetite. But don't imagine,' he added, detecting a look of dissatisfaction on Oblonsky's face, 'that I shan't appreciate your choice. I shall enjoy a good dinner.'

'I should hope so! Say what you like, it is one of the pleasures of life,' said Oblonsky, 'Well then, my good fellow, bring us two – no, three – dozen oysters, clear soup with vegetables . . .'

'*Printanière*,' prompted the Tartar. But Oblonsky evidently did not care to allow him the satisfaction of giving the dishes their French names. 'Soup with vegetables in it, you know. Then turbot with thick sauce. After that . . . roast beef (and see that it is good). Followed by capons; and we will finish up with fruit salad.'

Remembering that Oblonsky would not call the dishes by their French names, the Tartar did not repeat the order after him but could not resist the pleasure of rehearsing it to himself according to the menu, '*Soupe printanière, turbot sauce Beaumarchais, poulard à l'estragon, macèdoine de fruits . . .*' and immediately, as if worked by springs, he laid down the bill of fare in one cardboard cover and, seizing another, the wine list, put it before Oblonsky. 'What shall we drink?'

'Anything you like, only not much. Champagne,' said Levin.

'What? To begin with? After all, why not? You like the white seal?'

'*Carte blanc*,' put in the Tartar.

'Yes, bring us that with the oysters, and then we'll see.'

'Certainly, sir. And what *vin de table*?'

'You can give us *Nuits* – no, better, the classic *Chablis*.'

'Yes, sir. And cheese – your special?'

'Oh yes, Parmesan. Or would you prefer some other kind?' 'No, it's all the same to me,' replied Levin, unable to repress a smile.

And the Tartar darted off, his coat-tails flapping over his broad hips.

Leo Tolstoy, *Anna Karenina* (1876).

'By Jove, Robinson, you fellows round this town who have ruined your digestions with high living, have no notion of the zest with which a man can sit down to a few potato peelings, or a bit of broken pie crust, or—'

'Talk about hard food,' interrupted the other, 'I guess I know all about that. Many's the time I've breakfasted off a little cold porridge that somebody was going to throw away from a back-door, or that I've gone round to a livery stable and begged a little bran mash that they intended for the pigs. I'll venture to say I've eaten more hog's food—'

'Hog's food!' shouted Robinson, striking his fist savagely on the table, 'I tell you hog's food suits me better than—'

He stopped speaking with a sudden grunt of surprise as the waiter appeared with the question:

'What may I bring you for dinner, gentlemen?'

'Dinner!' said Jones, after a moment silence, 'dinner! Oh, anything, nothing – I never care what I eat – give me a little cold porridge, if you've got it, or a chunk of salt pork – anything you like, it's all the same to me.'

The waiter turned with an impassive face to Robinson.

'You can bring me some of that cold porridge too,' he said, with a defiant look at Jones; 'yesterday's if you have it, and a few potato peelings and a glass of skim milk.'

There was a pause. Jones sat back in his chair and looked hard across at Robinson. For some moments the two men gazed into each other's eyes with a stern, defiant intensity. Then Robinson turned slowly round in his seat and beckoned to the waiter, who was moving off with the muttered order on his lips.

'Here, waiter,' he said with a savage scowl, 'I guess I'll change that order a little. Instead of that cold porridge I'll take – um, yes – a little hot partridge. And you might as well bring me an oyster or two on the half shell, and a mouthful of soup (mock-turtle, consommé, anything), and perhaps you might fetch along a dab of fish, and a little peck of Stilton, and a grape, or a walnut.

The waiter turned to Jones.

'I guess I'll take the same,' he said simply, and added, 'and you might bring a quart of champagne at the same time.'

Stephen Leacock, *Literary Lapses* (1910).

Then, of course, there is the cosy type of tea-shop run on amateur lines where genteel young women who do not seem to have forgotten William Morris bend wistfully over the meringues in brown or sage green *crêpe de Chine* gowns and an air of shattered romance. Such places have fanciful names designed to attract those with a passion for peace. They are always just opening or going smash, and there is a widespread belief in the suburbs among enterprising young women that think this is the way to an enormous bank account.

'Thanks awfully!'

That's what they say when you pay the bill, and such a sad, sweet smile goes with it. Andromeda chained to a cheese cake.

H.V. Morton, *The Heart of London* (1923).

Another periodical of the same year has a reference to the new and strange fashion which permitted 'ladies' to take after-theatre suppers in restaurants. A very Country woman asks her military son to take her somewhere for supper – some place where a woman can go with propriety. The answer is – where, at that hour of the night, could they go without impropriety? But then he remembers that in the changed times women of the highest rank may go almost anywhere without impropriety. He suggests a place near Haymarket – Wilcocks's – with a warning that it will have mixed company; 'actresses and that sort of thing'; but immediately adds that everybody goes to Wilcocks's – Everybody – the Marchioness of— and Lady— were there the other night, and without escort. So they go, and take a 'light' supper – fried kidneys, sausage, cold duck, fried potatoes, cherry tart and cream, Stilton, and champagne.

Thomas Burke, *English Night Life* (1941).

Ezra listened to the customer – or a one-time customer, from the sound of it. 'Used to be,' the man was saying, 'this place had class. You follow me?'

Ezra nodded, watching him with such a sympathetic, kindly expression that Cody wondered if his mind weren't somewhere else altogether. 'Used to be there was fine French cuisine, flamed at the tables and all,' said the man. 'And chandeliers. And a hat-check girl. And waiters in black tie. What happened to your waiters?'

'They put people off,' Ezra said. 'They seemed to thing the customers were taking an exam of some sort, not just ordering a meal. They were uppish.'

'I liked your waiters.'

'Nowadays our staff is homier,' Ezra said, and he gestured towards a passing waitress – a tall, stooped, colourless girl, open mouthed with concentration, fiercely intent upon the coffee mug that she carried in both hands. She inched across the floor, breathing adenoidally.

Anne Tyler, Dinner at the Homesick Restaurant (1982).

There comes before me a vision of certain vegetarian restaurants, where, at a minim outlay, I have often enough made believe to satisfy my craving stomach; where I have swallowed 'savory cutlet,' 'vegetable steak,' and I know not what windy insufficiencies tricked up under specious names. One place I do recall where you had a complete dinner for sixpence – I dare not try and remember the items. But well indeed do I see the faces of the guests – poor clerks and shop-boys, bloodless girls and women of many sorts – all endeavouring to find a relish in lentil soup and haricot something-or-other. It was a grotesquely heart-breaking sight.

George Gissing, The Private Papers of Henry Ryecroft (1903).

'Food on board'

Another fellow I know went for a week's voyage round the coast, and, before they started, the steward came to him to ask whether he would pay for each meal as he had it, or arrange beforehand for the whole series. The steward recommended the latter course, as it would come to so much cheaper. He said they would do him for the whole week at two-pounds-five. He said for breakfast there would be fish, followed by a grill. Lunch was at one, and consisted of four courses. Dinner at six – soup, fish, entrée, joint, poultry, salad, sweets, cheese and desert. And a light supper at ten. My friend thought he would close on the two-pounds-five job (he is a hearty eater), and did so. Lunch came just as they were off Sheerness. He didn't feel so hungry as he thought he should, and so contented himself with a bit of boiled beef, and some strawberries and cream. He pondered a good deal during the afternoon, and at one time it seemed to him that he had been eating nothing but boiled beef for weeks, and at other times it seemed that he must have been living on strawberries and cream for years. Neither the beef nor the strawberries and cream seemed happy, either – seemed discontented like. At six, they came and told him dinner was ready. The announcement aroused no enthusiasm within him, but he felt that there was some of that two-pounds-five to work off, and he held on to ropes and things and went down. A pleasant odour of onions and hot ham, mingled with fried fish and greens, greeted him at the bottom of the ladder; and then the stewards came up with an oily smile, and said: 'What can I get you, sir?'

'Get me out of this,' was the feeble reply. And they ran him up quick, and propped him up, over to leeward, and left him. For the next four days he lived a simple and blameless life on thin Captain's biscuits (I mean that the biscuits were thin, not the captain) and soda-water; but, towards Saturday, he got uppish, and went in for weak tea and dry toast, then on Monday he was gorging himself on chicken broth. He left the ship on Tuesday, and as it steamed away from the landing-stage he gazed after it regretfully. 'There she goes,' he said, 'there she goes, with two pounds' worth of food on board that belongs to me, and that I haven't had.'

Jerome K. Jerome, *Three Men in a Boat* (1889).

I travelled to town with a family of children who ate without intermission from Market Harborough, where they got into the coach, to the Peacock at Islington, where they got out of it. They breakfasted as if they had fasted all the preceding day. They dined as if they had never breakfasted. They ate on the road one large basket of sandwiches, another of fruit, and a boiled fowl: besides which there was not an orange-girl, and old man with cakes, or a boy with filberts, who came to the coach-side when we stopped to change horses, of whom they did not buy something.

Thomas Babington Macaulay, letter to Hannah Macaulay, 20 September, 1832.

A little while ago I happened to be dining in the train; and I am very fond of dining in the train – or, indeed anywhere else. I know that people sometimes write to the papers, or even make scenes in the railway carriage, complaining of the railway dinner service; but my complaint was quite different – and indeed, quite contrary. I did not complain of the dinner because it was too bad, but because it was too good. The pleasure of eating in trains is akin to the pleasure of picnics, and should have a character adapted to its abnormal and almost adventurous conditions. This dinner was what is called a good dinner – that is it was about as twice as long as any normal person would want in his own home, and a great deal longer than he would want even in an ordinary restaurant. The train was also what is called a good train – that is, it was a train that swayed wildly from side to side in hurtling through England like a thunderbolt. Nobody who really wanted to enjoy a long and luxurious dinner would dream of sitting down to it under those conditions. Nobody would desire the restaurant tables to be shot round and round the restaurant like a giddy-go-round. Anybody would see in the abstract that it is foolish to attempt to possess simultaneously the advantage of luxury and leisure with the other advantage of speed. It is merely paying for a luxury and purchasing an inconvenience. Add to this the fact that, though the dinner was long, the time given for it was short. For there were other eager epicures waiting to be flung against windows while balancing asparagus or dissecting sardines. Other happy gourmets were to have the opportunity of spilling their soup and upsetting their coffee on that careering vehicle.

G.K. Chesterton, 'On Pleasure-seeking' (1939).

From the pocket of his overcoat he pulled out a large and dampish parcel of whose existence my nose had long made me aware. 'Guess what's in here.'

'Prawns,' I said, without an instant's hesitation.

And prawns it was, a whole kilo of them. And there we sat in opposite corners of our first-class carriage, with the little folding table opened out between us and the pink prawns on the table, eating with infinite relish and throwing the rosy carapaces, the tails, and the sucked heads out of the window. And the Flemish plain moved past us; the long double files of poplars, planted along the banks of the canals, of the fringes of the high roads, moving as we moved, marched parallel with our course or present, as we crossed them at right angles, for one significant flashing moment the entrance to Hobbema's avenue. And now the belfries of Bruges beckoned from far off across the plain; a dozen more shrimps and we were roaring through its station, all gloom and ogives in honour of Memling and the Gothic past. By the time we had eaten another hectogram of prawns, the modern quarter of

Ghent was reminding us that art was only five years old and had been invented in Vienna. At Alost the factor chimneys smoked; and before we knew where we were, we were almost on the outskirts of Brussels, with two or three hundred grammes of sea-fruit still intact on the table before us.

'Hurry up!' cried my Uncle Spencer, threatened by another access of anxiety. 'We must finish them before we get to Brussels.'

And during the last five miles we ate furiously, shell and all; there was hardly time even to spit out the heads and tails. 'Nothing like prawns,' my Uncle Spencer never failed to say, as the express drew slowly into the station at Brussels, and the last tails and whiskers with the fishy paper were thrown out of the window.

Aldous Huxley, 'Uncle Spencer' (1924).

'Rude comments on skool food'

Food at the High School could not have been more different than the Convent's. Coming into the dining hall for breakfast, lunch and supper the room glimmered with whiteness, for a glass of full-cream milk stood at every place, and on each table were several platters of thinly cut white bread spread with glistening white butter. At breakfast, white mealiemeal porridge and white sugar, white bread and golden syrup. At lunch, cold meat and boiled potatoes, then 'cake' pudding with jam. At supper, macaroni cheese and white bread and butter. Once a week we had an orange, once a week a bit of lettuce. We learned a useful lesson in the ways of the world, because we knew when the food inspector was coming, for as we entered the dining room there would be an egg or a jelly. In fact, white bread and butter was the staple of our diet. Years later, when I compared notes with a fellow sufferer, we agreed this was the only time in our lives we had been constipated. And we were always hungry. We ate nasturtium leaves, we spread mustard on the bread, and we begged food parcels from home like refugees.

Doris Lessing, *Under My Skin* (1994).

At Prep School in those days, a parcel of tuck was sent once a week by anxious mothers to their ravenous little sons, and an average tuck-box would probably contain, at almost any time, half a home-made currant cake, a packet of squashed-fly biscuits, a couple of oranges, an apple, a banana, a pot of strawberry jam or Marmite, a bar of chocolate, a bag of Liquorice Allsorts and a tin of Bassett's lemonade powder. An English school in those days was a purely money-making business owned and operated by the Headmaster. It suited him, therefore, to give the boys as little food as possible himself and to encourage their parents in various cunning ways to feed their offspring by parcel-post from home.

Roald Dahl, *Boy* (1984).

Mrs Young had informed us how nutritious and well-balanced school meals were. It was a point that would be rubbed in by later teachers. There was a kind of hidden implication that we were all fed on shit at home. Because we were there on the same day each week, school dinners were fairly constant. The part we liked was the dessert. It was almost always squares of rice crispies congealed together with melted chocolate. The first course was usually fish fried in breadcrumbs, a stewed tomato and grey boiled potatoes. The fish was even less fresh than Mr. Cope's was, but it was the tomato I found really offensive. It was the first of many occasions when I begged my mother to write a note to have me excused from one or other food item. Every crumb of a school dinner had to be eaten. Haberdashers' had an inflexible rule about it. We were all watched to make sure every nauseous mouthful went down. This meal was relatively inoffensive compared with some were expected to eat in the coming years. Quite why any school should consider it morally valuable to force kids to eat every morsel of things that disgust them I have never been able to understand. Surely, in adult life, it's a man or woman's taste and discrimination about food and other things that mark him out from the beasts. Yet, in the years that followed we were supposed to feast and be grateful for whatever nasty slop of overcooked titbit was set before us. Every scrap of fat on the meat was supposed to be eaten in the cause of discipline and 'good nutrition', likewise lumps of black in potatoes that had gone bad.

Fiona Pitt-Kethley, *My Schooling* (2002).

We then sat down to a meal which Dante would have hesitated to invent. I was seated opposite my parents, between a spherical house matron and a silent French *assistant*. The first course was a soup in which pieces of undisguised and unabashed gristle floated in a mud-coloured sauce whose texture and temperature were powerfully reminiscent of mucus. Then a steaming vat was placed in the middle of the table, where the jowly, watch-chained headmaster presided. He plunged his serving arm into the vessel and emerged with a ladleful of hot food, steaming like fresh horse dung on a cold morning. For a heady moment I thought I was going to be sick. A plate of *soi-disant* cottage pie – the mince grey, the potato beige – was set in front of me.

John Lanchester, *The Debt to Pleasure* (1996).

Many boys find themselves quiet incapable of making any rude comments on skool food. This is hardly good maners hem-hem and i must impress on all cads and bounders who sa poo gosh when they see a skool sossage to mend their ways.

When faced with a friteful piece of meat which even the skool dog would refuse do not screw up the face in any circs and sa coo ur gosh ghastly. This calls attention to oneself and makes it more difficult to pinch a beter piece from the next boy.

Geoffrey Willans, *The Compleet Molesworth* (1958).

8. GOING WITHOUT

'Never quite enough to go round'

ALGERNON: You can't possibly ask me to go without having some dinner. It's absurd. I never go without my dinner. No one ever does, except vegetarians and people like that.

Oscar Wilde, *The Importance of Being Earnest* (1895).

It is hard to go without one's dinner through sheer distress, but harder still to go without one's breakfast. Upon the strength of that first and aboriginal meal, one may muster courage to face the difficulties before one, and to dare the worst: but to be roused out of one's warm bed, and perhaps a profound oblivion of care, with golden dreams (for poverty does not prevent golden dreams), and told there is nothing for breakfast, is cold comfort for which one's half-strung nerves are not prepared, and throws a damp upon the prospects of the day. It is a bad beginning.

William Hazlitt, 'On the Want of Money' (1827).

I'm afraid I must ask you to step outside and . . . make the toast.

She rolled out of bed and began to get dressed. Okay, she said, But only cause I'm wasting away waiting for you to do it.

Why else?

She smiled at him, stuck up two fingers, and left the room.

He listened to her walking away, then laughed to himself and lay back across the bed, putting his hands behind his head as she had done earlier and laughing again. Then he sighed, smiling.

The door banged open and she strode into the room. Shit! There's no milk.

So? He sat up. We've had it black before.

There's no bread either.

What? There were at least two slices there last night! Has somebody nicked it? I wouldn't put it past that bastard next door . . .

No, shut up, listen: it's mouldy, that's all.

He shrugged. Cut the bad bits off them.

It's all fucking bad bits! she shouted. If I cut the bad bits off we'll be left with two toasted crumbs for our Sunday breakfast!

He creased his forehead. What've we got then?

She leaned back against the wall, her eyes closed. Some lentils.

And?

That's about it really. There's that Chinese seaweed you bought. Pity you hadn't bought some kippers instead. Mind you they'd smell pretty bad by now seeing as you've had the bloody stuff for six months and never used it once.

I'm just waiting to find a recipe, he said quietly.

Duncan McLean, 'Shoebox' (1992).

Several days after my visit to the music store, a minor disaster nearly drowned me. The two eggs I was about to place in a pot of water and boil up for my daily meal slipped through my fingers and broke on the floor. Those were the last two eggs of my current supply, and I could not help feeling that this was the cruellest, most terrible thing that had ever happened to me. The eggs landed with an ugly splat. I remember standing there in horror as they oozed out over the floor. The sunny, translucent innards sank into the cracks, and suddenly there was muck everywhere, a bobbing slush of slime and shell. One yolk had miraculously survived the fall, but when I bent down to scoop it up, it slid out from under the spoon and broke apart. I felt as though a star were exploding, as though a great sun had just died.

Paul Auster, *Moon Palace* (1989).

The boots are behind the kitchen door. Anna lifts them. They're heavier than boots should be. She puts her hand into the right boot, and her touch meets cold glass. She draws out a small pot of jam, labelled in Marina's bold, spear-like hand-writing: *Raspberry jam 1940*. She reaches into the left boot, and there, too, is a jar. This time, the jam is cloudberry. They are small jars, holding about four hundred grammes each. How has Marina done it> How has she had the strength to hold these back?

'Marina!'

'Bring it here. We'll have tea with jam. But this is the last of it, Anna, it's all I've got. I hid them away. But now's the time to eat it, because it won't get any worse than this.'

'What is it, Anna?' calls Kolya, looking at his sister in the doorway, her face blazing, tears sliding down her cheeks as she holds up the two jars of jam, one in each fist, like a boxer in triumph after the last, bloody, flesh-pulping round.

'Jam.'

'Jam!'

They swoop on Marina, clutching her, hugging one another, on their knees and tangled in blanket. Kolya butts his head into Marina's lap. 'Jam, jam, jam!' He shoves against her. He claws at her clothes. 'Jam, Marina! Jam!'

'Look, raspberry jam!' Anna holds it up to the light and the seeds hang like points of straw in ruby flesh.

'And cloudberry . . .' says Andrei. 'Cloudberry – it's my favourite.'

They don't dare talk about the food of the past, though they're obsessed by it. Each one of them is locked in silent, separate craving. Little savoury pastries packed with jelly and rich meat. Blinis with red caviar and white sour cream. 'That ice-cream I had last summer – and I didn't even finish it.' And the ice-cream marches across your mind to torment you. Chocolate Eskimo, glistening, rich with cream and sugar, scented with vanilla, sliding across the tongue, dripping to the ground, half of it wasted, not even thought about – how could you have done that?

Helen Dunmore, *The Siege* (2001).

More than once during his life in the camps, Shukhov had recalled the way they used to eat in his village: whole saucepans of potatoes, pots of porridge and, in the early days, big chunks of meat. And milk enough to split their guts. That wasn't the way to eat, he learned in camp. You had to eat with all your mind on the food – like now, nibbling the bread bit by bit, working the crumbs up into a paste with your tongue and sucking it into your cheeks. And how good it tasted, that soggy black bread!

Alexander Solzhenitsyn, *One Day in the Life of Ivan Denisovich* (1962).

Jack ate against time, that was really his secret; and in our house you had to do it. Imagine us all sitting down to dinner; eight round a pot of stew. It was lentil-stew usually, heavy brown mash made apparently of plastic studs. Though it smelt of hot stables, we were used to it, and it was filling enough – could you get it. But the size of our family out-stripped the size of the pot, so there was never quite enough to go round.

Laurie Lee, *Cider with Rosie* (1959).

He smiles, and then he does a strange thing. He puts his left hand into his pocket and pulls out an apple. He walks over to me slowly, holding the apple out in front of him like someone holding out a bone to a dangerous dog, in order to win it over.

This is for you, he says.

I am so thirsty the apple looks to me like a big round drop of water, cool and red. I could drink it down in one gulp. I hesitate; but then I think, There's nothing bad in an apple, and so I take it. I haven't had an apple of my own for a long time. This apple must be from last autumn, kept in a barrel in the cellar, but it seems fresh enough.

I'm not a dog, I say to him.

Most people would ask me what I mean by saying that, but he laughs. His laugh is just one breath, Hah, as if he's found a thing he had lost; and he says, No, Grace, I can see you are not a dog.

What is he thinking? I stand and hold the apple in both hands. It feels precious, like a heavy treasure. I lift it up and smell it. It has such an odour of outdoors on it I want to cry.

Aren't you going to eat it, he says.

No, not yet, I say.

Why not, he says.

Because then it would be gone, I say.

Margaret Atwood, *Alias Grace* (1997).

The members of this board were very sage, deep, philosophical men; and when they came to turn their attention to the workhouse, they found out at once, what ordinary folks would never have discovered – the poor people liked it! It was a regular place of public entertainment for the poorer classes; a tavern where there was nothing to pay; a public breakfast, dinner, tea, and supper all the year round; a brick and mortar elysium, where it was all play and no work.

'Oho!' said the board, looking very knowing; 'we are the fellows to set this to rights; we'll stop it all, in no time.' So, they established the rule, that all poor people should have the alternative (for they would compel nobody, not they), of being starved by a gradual process in the house, or by a quick one out of it. With this view, they contracted with the water-works to lay on an unlimited supply of water; and with a corn-factor to supply periodically small quantities of oatmeal; and issued three meals of thin gruel a day, with an onion twice a week, and half a roll of Sundays.

Charles Dickens, *Oliver Twist* (1838).

'What's wrong with the Gospels, Father?'
'They make no sense,' the ex-priest said, 'anyway not in Paraguay. "Sell all and give to the poor" – I had to read that out to them while the old Archbishop we had in those days was eating a fine fish from Iguazu and drinking a French wine with the General.'

Graham Greene, *The Honorary Consul* (1973).

Love and business and family and religion and art and patriotism are nothing but shadows of words when a man is starving.

O. Henry, 'Cupid à la Carte', *Heart of the West* (1907).

'Of a thrifty nature'

I am one of those, who freely and ungrudgingly impart a share of the good things of this life which fall to their lot (few as mine are in this kind) to a friend. I protest I take as great an interest in my friend's pleasures, his relishes, and proper satisfactions, as my own. 'Presents,' I often say, 'endear Absents.'

Hares, pheasants, partridges, snipes, barn-door chickens, (those 'tame villatic fowl'), capons, plovers, brawn, barrels of oysters, I dispense as freely as I receive them. I love to taste them, as it were, upon the tongue of my friend. But a stop must be put somewhere. One would not, like Lear, 'give everything.' I make my stand upon pig.

Charles Lamb, 'A Dissertation upon Roast Pig' (1823).

23. Whoso is liberal of his meat men shall speak well of him; and the report of his good housekeeping will be believed.

24. But against him that is a niggard of his meat the whole city shall murmur; and the testimonies of his niggardness shall not be doubted of.

Ecclesiasticus, xxxi, 23–4.

A lady of my family went to live in a friend's house in the friend's absence; to be waited on by a sort of superior servant. The lady had got it fixed in her head that the servant cooked her own meals separately, whereas the servant was equally fixed on the policy of eating what was left over from the lady's meals. The servant sent up for breakfast, say, five rashers of bacon; which was more than the lady wanted. But the lady had another fixed freak of conscience common in the ladies of the period. She thought nothing should be wasted; and could not see that even a thing consumed is wasted if it is not wanted. She ate the five rashers and the servant consequently sent up seven rashers. The lady paled a little, but followed the path of duty and ate them all. The servant, beginning to feel that she too would like a little breakfast, sent up nine or ten rashers. The lady, rallying all her powers, charged at them with her head down, and swept them from the field. And so, I suppose, it went on; owing to the polite silence between the two social classes. I dare not think how it ended.

The logical conclusion would seem to be that the servant starved and the lady burst.

G.K Chesterton, *Autobiography* (1937).

Being of a thrifty nature, she ate slowly, picking up from the table the crumbs from her loaf of bread – a twelve pound loaf which was baked specially for her and lasted her twenty days.

Gustave Flaubert, 'A Simple Heart' (1875).

When the guests arrive he goes unctuously to the cupboard and gets out the dry crusts of breads which he toasted maybe a week ago and which taste strongly now of the mouldy wood. Not a crumb is thrown away. If the bread gets too sour he takes it downstairs to the concierge who, so he says, has been very kind to him. According to him, the concierge is delighted to get the stale bread – she makes bread and butter pudding with it.

Henry Miller, *The Tropic of Cancer* (1963).

Here was my soup. Dinner was being served in the great dining-hall. Far from being spring it was in fact an evening in October. Everybody was assembled in the big dining-room. Dinner was ready. Here was the soup. It was a plain gravy soup. There was nothing to stir the fancy in that. One could have seen through the transparent liquid any pattern that there might have been on the plate itself. But there was no pattern. The plate was plain. Next came beef with its attendant greens and potatoes – a homely trinity, suggesting the rumps of cattle in a muddy market, and sprouts curled and yellowed at the edges, and bargaining and cheapening, and women with string bags on Monday morning. There was no reason to complain of human nature's daily food, seeing that the supply was sufficient and coal-miners doubtless were sitting down to less. Prunes and custard followed. And if any-one complains that prunes, even when mitigated by custard are an uncharitable vegetable (fruit they are not), stringy as a miser's heart and exuding a fluid such as might run in misers' veins who have denied themselves wine and warmth for eighty years and yet not given to the poor, he should reflect that there are people whose charity embraces even the prune. Biscuits and cheese came next, and here the water-jug was lib-erally passed round, for it is the nature of biscuits to be dry, and these were biscuits to the core. That was all. The meal was over.

Virginia Woolf, *A Room of One's Own* (1928).

I am remarkably fond of beans and bacon; and this fond-ness I attribute to my father having given me a penny for hav-ing eat a large quantity of beans on Saturday. For the other boys did not like them, and as it was an economic food, my father thought that my attachment and penchant for it should be encouraged.

Samuel Taylor Coleridge, letter to Thomas Poole, 9 October, 1797.

Her husband was mean. It was getting worse. After much brooding in the kitchen, sorting through the shelves and cup-boards, he denounced his wife as a wanton housekeeper. Too many jars, too many packets, too many tins. All shouting abundance, luxury, waste. There would be no more money until every last thing on the shelves was eaten. Now they were down to Sun Maid raisins and Sainsbury's Wheat Bisks. For three days the children had eaten only Wheat Bisks in water with handfuls of raisins. This will teach you, said the hus-band. Will teach you to buy Sun Maid, fancy packets, penny-waste here, penny-waste there.

Monica Ali, *Brick Lane* (2003).

9. MANNERS AND MORALS

'Rudimentary table manners'

On the Continent, people have good food; in England, people have good table manners.

George Mikes, *How to be an Alien* (1946).

She buttered her roll and ate. Miss Fisher, meanwhile, broke a croissant in two and dipped it with perfect naturalness into her coffee, smiling away to herself for some interior reason and not observing Henrietta's surprise. Henrietta was sure you did not do this with bread; travel had still to do much for her priggishness about table manners.

Elizabeth Bowen, *The House in Paris* (1935).

Conversation was impossible for a long time; and when it was slowly resumed, it was that regrettable sort of conversation that results from talking with your mouth full. The Badger did not mind that sort of thing at all, nor did he take any notice of elbows on the table, or everybody speaking at once. As he did not go into Society himself, he had got an idea that these things belonged to the things that didn't really matter. (We know of course that he was wrong, and took too narrow a view; because they do matter very much, though it would take too long to explain why.)

Kenneth Grahame, *The Wind in the Willows* (1908).

The impressive but somewhat forbidding person who announces (as if it were a verdict rather than an invitation) that 'dinner is served' or the master of ceremonies who, when dinner is over, intones the invocation of 'Pray silence', has a grand stand view of eating which can scarcely be shared by the diners or the waiters, who are both too busy. Glasses can be decently and even ceremoniously raised, and drink flows unnoticeably down the gullet; but to see a party of ladies and gentlemen ladling their soup, forking the meat into their gaping jaws like hay onto a hay-wagon, dangling their asparagus, or disposing of pips and stones with an absent-minded but guilty look, must tend to give an unkind view of human nature.

A. Goidel, *Alphabet for Odette* (1946).

Towards the end of dinner, and before the ladies retire, bowls of coloured glass full of water are placed before each person. All (women as well as men) stoop over it, sucking up some of the water, and returning it, perhaps more than once, and, with a spitting and washing sort of noise, quite charming, – the operation frequently assisted by a finger elegantly thrust into the mouth! All this done, and with the hands dipped also, the napkins, and sometimes the table-cloth, are used to wipe hand and mouth.

L. Simons, *Journal of a Tour and Residence in Great Britain during the Years 1810 and 1811* (1817).

'Mr Sampson is a man whom I esteem for his simplicity and benevolence of character.'

'Oh, I am convinced of his generosity too,' said this lively lady; 'he cannot lift a spoonful of soup to his mouth without bestowing a share on everything round.'

Walter Scott, *Guy Mannering* (1815).

Nantwich proved to be a voracious eater with poor table manners. Half the time he ate with his mouth open, affording me a generous view of masticated pork and apple sauce, which he smeared around his wine glass when he drank without wiping his lips.

Alan Hollinghurst, *The Swimming-pool Library* (1988).

When it came to serving, Mother had no method, not even the law of chance – a dab on each place in any old order and then every man for himself. No grace, no warning, no starting-gun; but the first to finish what he'd had on his plate could claim what was left in the pot. Mother's swooping spoon was breathlessly watched – let the lentils fall where they may. But starving Jack had worked it all out, he followed the spoon with his plate. Absentmindedly Mother would give him first dollop, and very often a second, and as soon as he got it he swallowed it whole, not using his teeth at all. 'More please, I've finished' – the bare plate proved it, so he got the pot-scrapings too.

Laurie Lee, *Cider with Rosie* (1959).

Spaghetti was one of Lin's favourite foods because it was both delicious and thought-provoking. They'd been coming to Rigazzi's for as long as he could remember, and his father had taught him how to twirl spaghetti on his fork, instead of cutting it up. The trick, he'd learned, was to start with just a few strands; otherwise you ended up with a big ball of pasta twine that either you couldn't fit in your mouth or gagged you when you tried to chew. Even though he now regarded himself as an expert twirler, he still liked it that you couldn't predict, when you pulled on one strand, which strand on the opposite side of the plate would snake toward you fork though the giant tangle. Even when you'd eaten most of it, you still couldn't tell what was connected to what. This complexity and surprise was nearly as delicious as the actual taste.

Richard Russo, 'The Mysteries of Linwood Hart' (2002).

Grim Silas Foster, all this while, had been busy at the supper-table, pouring out his own tea, and gulping it down with no more sense of its exquisiteness than if it were a decoction of catnip; helping himself to pieces of dipt toast on the flat of his knife-blade, and dropping half of it on the table-cloth; using the same serviceable implement to cut slice after slice of ham; perpetrating terrible enormities with the butter-plate; and, in all other respects, behaving less like a civilized Christian than the worst kind of an ogre.

Nathaniel Hawthorne, *The Blithedale Romance* (1852).

It was a wonderful dinner with real champagne (lovely, rather like very good ginger ale without the ginger). But I wish I could have had that food when I wasn't at a party, because you can't notice food fully when you are being polite. And I was a little bit nervous – the knives and forks were so complicated. I never expected to feel ignorant about such things – we always had several courses for dinner at Aunt Millicent's – but I couldn't even recognise all the dishes. And it was no use trying to copy Neil because his table manners were quite strange to me. I fear he must have seen me staring at him once because he said: 'Mother thinks I ought to eat in the English way – she and Simon have gotten into it – but I'm darned if I will.'

I asked him to explain the difference. It appears that in America it is polite to cut up each mouthful, lay down the knife on your plate, change your fork from the left to the right hand, load it, eat the fork-full, change the fork back to your left hand, and pick up the knife again – and you must take only one kind of food on the fork at a time; never a nice comfortable wodge of meat and vegetables together.

'But that takes so long,' I said.

'No, it doesn't,' said Neil. 'Anyway, it looks terrible the way you all hang on to your knives.'

The idea of anything English people do looking terrible quite annoyed me, but I held my peace.

Dodie Smith, *I Capture the Castle* (1949).

Wirf dove into the food hungrily.

'I don't think I can watch this,' Sully said, wondering how a man could get a degree in law without picking up some rudimentary table manners. Wirf forked with his left, knifed with his right, put neither utensil down until they were no longer of practical use.

Richard Russo, *Nobody's Fool* (1993).

When the ducks and green peas came, we looked at each other in dismay; we had only two-pronged, black-handled forks. It is true, the steel was as bright as silver; but what were we to do? Miss Matty picked up her peas, one by one, on the point of the prongs, much as Aminé ate her grains of rice after her previous feast with the Ghoul. Miss Pole sighted over her delicate young peas as she left them on one side of the plate untested; for they *would* drop between the prongs. I looked at my host: the peas were going up whole-sale into his capacious mouth, shovelled up by his large round-ended knife. I saw, I imitated, I survived! My friends, in spite of my precedent, could not muster up courage enough to do an ungenteel thing; and, if Mr Holbrook had not been so heartily hungry, he would prob-ably have seen that the good peas went away almost untouched.

Elizabeth Gaskell, *Cranford* (1853).

A tray was brought with everything upon it, even to the cucumber; and Mrs. Gamp accordingly sat down to eat and drink in high good humour. The extent to which she availed herself of the vinegar, and supped up that refreshing fluid with the blade of her knife, can scarcely be expressed in narrative.

Charles Dickens, *Martin Chuzzlewit* (1844).

The first time I went to an Indian restaurant in Canada I used my fingers. The waiter looked at me critically and said, 'Fresh off the boat, are you?' I blanched. My fingers, which a second before had been taste buds savouring the food a little ahead of my mouth, became dirty under his gaze. They froze like criminals caught in the act. I didn't dare lick them. I wiped them guiltily on my napkin. He had no idea how deeply those words wounded me. They were like nails being driven into my flesh. I picked up a knife and fork. I had hardly ever used such instruments. My hands trembled. My sambar lost its taste.

Yann Martel, *The Life of Pi* (2003).

16. Eat, as it becometh a man, those things which are set before thee; and devour not, lest thou be hated. Leave off first for manners' sake; and devour not, lest thou be hated.

17. Leave off first, for manners' sake; and be not unsatiable, lest thou offend.

18. When thou sittest among many, reach not thy hand out first of all.

Ecclesiasticus, xxxi, 16–18.

Queequeg sat there among them – at the head of the table, too, it so chanced; as cool as an icicle. To be sure I cannot say much for his breeding. His greatest admirer could not have cordially justified his bringing his harpoon into breakfast with him, and using it there without ceremony; reaching over the table with it, to the imminent jeopardy of many heads, and grappling the beefsteaks towards him. But *that* was certainly very coolly done by him, and every one knows that in most people's estimation, to do anything coolly is to do it genteelly.

Herman Melville, *Moby Dick* (1851).

'Quite capable of being a glutton'

When at last they were so thoroughly toasted, the Badger summoned them to the table, where he had been busy laying a repast. They had felt pretty hungry before, but when they actually saw at last the supper that was spread for them, really it seemed only a question of what they should attack first where all was so attractive, and whether the other things would obligingly wait for them till they had time to give them attention.

Kenneth Grahame, *The Wind in the Willows* (1908).

I was startled when the bill of fare was brought, for the prices were a great deal higher than I had anticipated. But she reassured me.

'I don't eat anything for luncheon,' she said.

'Oh, don't say that!' I answered generously.

'I never eat more than one thing. I think people eat far too much nowadays. A little fish, perhaps. I wonder if they have any salmon.'

Well, it was early in the year for salmon and it was not on the bill of fare, but I asked the waiter if there was any. Yes, a beautiful salmon had just come in, it was the first they had had. I ordered it for my guest. The waiter asked her if she would have something while it was being cooked.

'No,' she answered, 'I never eat more than one thing. Unless you had a little caviare. I never mind caviar.'

My heart sank a little. I knew I could not afford caviare,

but I could not very well tell her that. I told the waiter by all means to bring caviare. For myself I chose the cheapest dish on the menu and that was a mutton chop.

'I think you are unwise to eat meat,' she said. 'I don't know how you can expect to work after eating heavy things like chops. I don't believe in overloading my stomach.'

Then came the question of drink.

'I never drink anything for luncheon,' she said.

'Neither do I,' I answered promptly.

'Except for white wine,' she proceeded as though I had not spoken. 'These French wines are so light. They're wonderful for the digestion.'

'What would you like?' I asked, hospitable still, but not exactly effusive.

She gave me a bright and amicable flash of her white teeth.

'My doctor won't let me drink anything but champagne.'

I fancy turned a trifle pale. I ordered half a bottle. I mentioned casually that my doctor had absolutely forbidden me to drink champagne.

'What are you going to drink then?'

'Water.'

She ate the caviare and she ate the salmon. She talked gaily of art and literature and music. But I wondered what the bill would come to. When my mutton chop arrived she took me quiet seriously to task.

'I see that you're in the habit of eating a heavy luncheon. I'm sure it's a mistake. Why don't you follow my example and just eat one thing? I'm sure you'd feel every so much better for it.'

'I *am* only going to eat one thing,' I said, as the waiter came again with the bill of fare.

She waved him aside with an airy gesture.

'No, no, I never eat anything for luncheon. Just a bite, I never want more than that, and I eat that more as an excuse for conversation than anything else. I couldn't possible eat anything more – unless they had some of those giant asparagus. I should be sorry to leave Paris without having some of them.'

My heart sank. I had seen them in the shops and I knew that they were horrible expensive. My mouth had often watered at the sight of them.

'Madam wants to know if you have any of those giant asparagus,' I asked the waiter.

I tried with all my might to will him to say no. A happy smile spread over his broad, priest-like face, and he assured me that they had some so large, so splendid, so tender, that it was a marvel.

'I'm not in the least hungry,' my guest sighed, 'but if you insist I don't mind having some asparagus.'

I ordered them.

'Aren't you going to have any?'

'No, I never eat asparagus.'

'I know there are people who don't like them. The fact is, you ruin your palate by all the meat you eat.'

We waited for the asparagus to be cooked. Panic seized me. It was not a question now how much money I should have left over for the rest of the month, but whether I had enough to pay the bill. It would be mortifying to find myself ten francs short and be obliged to borrow from my guest. I could not bring myself to do that. I knew exactly how much I had and if the bill came to more I made up my mind that I would put my hand in my pocket and with a dramatic cry start up and say it had been picked. Of course it would be awkward if she had not money enough either to pay the bill. Then the only thing would be to leave my watch and say I would come back and pay later.

The asparagus appeared. They were enormous, succulent and appetising. The smell of the melted butter tickled my nostrils as the nostrils of Jehovah were tickled by the burned offering of the virtuous Semites. I watched the abandoned woman thrust them down her throat in large voluptuous mouthfuls and in my polite way I discoursed on the condition of the drama in the Balkans. At last she finished.

'Coffee?' I said.

'Yes, just an ice-cream and coffee,' she answered.

I was past caring now, so I ordered coffee for myself and an ice-cream and coffee for her.

'You know, there's one thing I thoroughly believe in,' she said, as she ate the ice-cream. 'One should always get up from a meal feeling one could eat a little more.'

'Are you still hungry?' I asked faintly.

'Oh no, I'm not hungry; you see, I don't eat luncheon. I have a cup of coffee in the morning and then dinner, but I never eat more than one thing for luncheon. I was speaking for you.'

'Oh, I see!'

Then a terrible thing happened. While we were waiting for the coffee, the head waiter, with an ingratiating smile on his false face, came up to us bearing a large basket full of huge peaches. They had the blush of an innocent girl; they had the rich tone of an Italian landscape. But surely peaches were not in season then? Lord knew what they cost. I knew too – a little later, for my guest, going on with her conversation, absentmindedly took one.

'You see, you've filled your stomach with a lot of meat' – my one miserable little chop – 'and you can't eat any more. But I've just had a snack and I shall enjoy a peach.'

The bill came and when I paid it I found that I had only enough for a quite inadequate tip. Her eyes rested for an instant on the three francs I left for the waiter and I knew that she thought me mean. But when I walked out of the restaurant I had the whole month before me and not a penny in my pocket.

'Follow my example,' she said as we shook hands, 'and never eat more than one thing for luncheon.'

'I'll do better than that,' I retorted. 'I'll eat nothing for dinner to-night.'

'Humorist!' she cried gaily, jumping into a cab. 'You're quite a humorist!'

But I had my revenge at last. I do not believe that I am a vindictive man, but when the immortal gods take a hand in the matter it is pardonable to observe the result with complacency. To-day she weighs twenty-one stone.

W. Somerset Maugham, 'The Luncheon' (1951).

On Wednesday night I always take my wife to the Chinese restaurant in the village, and then we go to the movies. We order the family dinner for two, but my wife eats most of it. She's a big eater. She reaches right across the table and grabs my egg roll, empties the roast duck onto her plate, takes my fortune-cookie away from me, and then when she's done she sighs a deep sigh and says, 'Well, you certainly stuffed yourself.'

John Cheever, 'The Chimera' (1946).

I have never been anything so refined as a gourmet: so I am happy to say that I am still quite capable of being a glutton. My ignorance of cookery is such that I can even eat the food in the most fashionable and expensive hotels in London.

G. K. Chesterton, *Autobiography* (1937).

Pooh always liked a little something at eleven o'clock in the morning, and he was very glad to see Rabbit getting out the plates and mugs; and when Rabbit said, 'Honey or condensed milk with your bread?' he was so excited that he said, 'Both,' and then, so as not to seem greedy, he added, 'But don't bother about the bread, please.' And for a long time after that he said nothing . . . until at last, humming to himself in a rather sticky voice, he got up, shook Rabbit lovingly by, the paw, and said that he must be going on.

'Must you?' said Rabbit politely.

'Well,' said Pooh, 'I could stay a little longer if it – if you –' and he tried very hard to look in the direction of the larder.

'As a matter of fact,' said Rabbit, 'I was going out myself directly.'

'Oh well, then, I'll be going on. Good-bye.'

'Well, good-bye, if you're sure you won't have any more.'

'Is there any more?' asked Pooh quickly.

Rabbit took the covers off the dishes, and said, 'No, there wasn't.'

'I thought not,' said Pooh, nodding to himself.

A.A. Milne, *Winnie the Pooh* (1926).

After a little while Nurse Matilda said: 'There's no need to gobble.'

But they did gobble. They always gobbled. They liked breakfast. They liked their porridge so stiff that it would spin round in its own milk like a little island. They liked to write their names, each on his own island of porridge, with a thin thread of treacle dripping from the spoon. And they like their boiled eggs, and turned them upside down in the egg-cups when they'd finished, to look like whole new eggs; and they liked their mugs of milk or tea, and their lovely fresh home-made bread and butter. So they went on gobbling: snatching bread and butter from under one another's noses, scooping out the last of the jam without caring who else wanted it, holding out their mugs for more, without a 'Please' or 'Thank you' . . .

Nurse Matilda sat at the top of the table, her big black stick in her hand. Down went the porridge, down went the eggs, down went the bread and butter and jam.

And more bread and butter and jam.

And *more* bread and butter and jam.

And *more* bread and butter and jam and more bread and butter and ham and MORE and MORE and MORE bread and butter and jam . . .

'Here,' said the children with their mouths full, 'that's enough!' only their mouths were so full that what they said sounded like 'Assawuff', and Nurse Matilda only looked politely puzzled and said, 'Did you ask for more porridge?' and to every child's horror, there before it was a plate of porridge all over again, spinning dizzily with its golden signature in its sea of milk. And their hands seized up their spoons and down went the porridge, stuff, stuff, stodge, stodge, on top of all that bread and butter. And suddenly all those upside-down eggshells really were full, new eggs; and up and down flashed their egg-spoons choking down egg on top of porridge; and on top of the egg came more and more of that dreadful bread and butter and jam . . . and then the porridge started all over again.

Christianna Brand, *Nurse Matilda* (1964).

The little boy, too, we observed, had a famous appetite, and consumed *Schinken,* and *Braten,* and *Kartoffeln,* and cranberry jam, and salad, and pudding, and roast fowls, and sweetmeats, with a gallantry that did honour to his nation. After about fifteen dishes, he concluded the repast with dessert, some of which he even carried out of doors, for some young gentlemen at table, amused with his coolness and gallant free-and-easy manner, induced him to pocket a handful of macaroons, which he discussed on his way to the theatre, whither everybody went in the cheery social little German place. The lady in black, the boy's mamma, laughed and blushed, and looked exceedingly pleased and shy as the dinner went on, and at the various feats and instances of *espieglerie* on the part of her son. The Colonel – for so he became very soon afterwards – I remember joked the boy with a great deal of grave fun, pointing out dishes which he hadn't tried, and entreating him not to baulk his appetite, but to have a second supply of this or that.

William Makepeace Thackeray, *Vanity Fair* (1847).

In 1798 I was at Versailles as a commissioner of the Directory, and had fairly frequent dealings with Monsieur Lapert, who was extremely fond of oysters, and used to complain of never having eaten enough of them, or as he put it, 'had his bellyful of them'.

I decided to provide him with that satisfaction, and to that end invited him to dinner. He came; I kept him company as far as the third dozen, after which I let him go on alone. He went up to thirty-two dozen, taking more than an hour over the task, for the servant was not very skilful at opening them.

Meanwhile, I was inactive, and as that is a distressing condition to be in at the table, I stopped my guest when he was still in full career. 'My dear fellow,' I said, 'it is not your fate to eat your bellyful of oysters today; let us have dinner.'

We dined: and he acquitted himself with the vigour and appetite of a man who had been fasting.

Jean-Anthelme Brillat-Savarin, *The Physiology of Taste* (1825).

Talking about eating, Madame Bergeret said that in Midi (neighbourhood of Toulouse especially) there used to be men who prided themselves on enormous powers of eating. They did not usually eat a great deal, but on occasions, when put to it, they would perform terrible feats such as consuming a whole turkey. The result sometimes was that they were very ill. The method of curing them was to dig a hole in the muck-heap, strip the sufferer naked, put him in the hole, and pack him tightly with manure up to his neck. The people who did this did it with gusto, telling the sufferer what an odious glutton he was. The heat generated promoted digestion in a manner almost miraculous, and next day the sufferer was perfectly restored.

Arnold Bennett, diary entry, 19 July, 1907.

Pie races were the most fun. Aunt Betts would cut great wedges of pie for Almedy and the children. Then she would set three pies in hot tins down on the table, their berry juice still bubbling up through the flaky white crusts. Aunt Betts and Uncle Louie, each with a knife in hand and shaking with suppressed glee, would eye each other steadily for a moment, then cry out together, 'Go!' Then their knives laid into the nearest pie, scooping it into their mouths, seeing who would get to the middle pie first. Uncle Louie always won because Aunt Betts got out of breath from laughing and had to unloose her belt, even her collar. One night they finished the cider barrel between them, drinking from the bung, and they must have had a race on the pantry too, for the fried squirrels and the corn pudding were all gone by morning.

Dawn Powell, *My Home is Far Away* (1944).

'Murder is justified'

Don't eat with your ears! By this I mean do not aim at having extraordinary out-of-the-way foods, just to astonish your guests.

Yuan Mei, 'The Art of Dining' (eighteenth century).

'I'd like to start with caviar and then have a plain grilled *rognon de veau* with *pommes soufflés*. And then I'd like to have *fraises des bois* with a lot of cream. Is it very shameless to be so certain and so expensive?' She smiled at him enquiringly. 'It's a virtue, and anyway it's only a good plain wholesome meal.' He turned to the maitre *d'hotel,* 'and bring plenty of toast.' 'The trouble always is,' he explained to Vesper, 'not how to get enough caviar, but how to get enough toast with it.' 'Now,' he turned back to the menu, 'I myself will accompany Mademoiselle with the caviar, but then I would like a very small *tournedos,* underdone, with *sauce Béarnaise* and a *coeur d'artichaut.* While Mademoiselle is enjoying the strawberries, I will have half an avocado pear with a little French dressing. Do you approve?' The maitre d'hotel bowed.

Ian Fleming, *Casino Royale* (1953).

Talking of potatoes, here's a gambit that you must look out for. Murder is justified in the circumstances.

Two men go into a restaurant. One of them picks up the menu idly and says *Oh good! There are new potatoes on the card today!*

The other man doesn't seem to understand and says *I beg your pardon?*

New potatoes, the first man says, *only a shilling extra.*

The other now looks genuinely puzzled. He searches his friend's face. *I'm afraid I don't quite get you,* he says. *Exactly what do you mean? New potatoes?*

Naturally this leads to some exasperation. *I see there are new potatoes on the card today, that's all,* the first man says rather shortly.

New … potatoes?

The second man has now built up a pucker of frowns on his face to show that he is completely at sea. He stares, lost. Then slowly … very slowly … light is seen to break. He has a clue. He grasps at it. Soon the meaning of his friend's remark is flooding out upon him. His face becomes smooth. He smiles.

Oh . . . I get you. Of course. New potatoes . . .

Here there is a carefully nursed pause.

We have had them at home, of course, for the last three months. St Patrick's Day I think, we had the first.

Another brief pause.

They were a bit late this year, of course. Last year it was about the first of March we had them, I think . . .

(It's at the second pause you use the gun.)

Flann O'Brien, *The Best of Myles* (1993).

'Did you have any trouble getting reservations at Propheteers?' I ask cutting him off.

'No. None at all,' he says. 'We ate late.'

'What did you order?' I ask.

'I had the poached oysters, the lotte and the walnut tart.'

'I hear the lotte is good there,' I murmur, lost in thought.

'The client had the boudin blanc, the roasted chicken and the cheesecake,' he says.

'Cheesecake?' I say, confused by this plain, alien-sounding list. 'What sauce or fruits were on the roasted chicken? What shapes was it cut into?'

'None, Patrick,' he says, also confused. 'It was . . . roasted.'

'And the cheesecake, what flavour? Was it heated?' I say. 'Ricotta cheesecake? Goat cheese? Were there flowers or cilantro in it?'

'It was just . . . regular,' he says, and then, 'Patrick you are sweating.'

'What did she have?' I ask, ignoring him. 'The client's bimbo.'

'Well, she had the country salad, the scallops and the lemon tart,' Luis says.

'The scallops were grilled? Where the sashimi scallops? In a ceviche of sorts?' I'm asking. 'Or were they *gratinized*?'

'No Patrick,' Luis says. 'They were . . . broiled.

It's silent in the boardroom as I contemplate this, thinking it through before asking, finally. 'What's "broiled," Luis?'

'I'm not sure,' he says. 'I think it involves . . . a pan.'

Bret Easton Ellis, *American Psycho* (1991).

'What is a Dinner-giving Snob?' some innocent youth, who is not répandu in the world, may ask, of some simple reader who has not the benefits of London society.

My dear sir, I will show you – not all, for that is impossible – several kinds of Dinner-giving Snobs. For instance, suppose you, in the middle rank of life, accustomed to mutton, roast on Tuesday, cold on Wednesday, hashed on Thursday, etc., with some small means and a small establishment, choose to waste the former and set the latter topsy-turvy by giving entertainments unnaturally costly – you come into the Dinner-giving Snob class at once. Suppose you get in cheap-made dishes from the pastrycook's, and hire a couple of green-grocers or carpet-beaters, to figure as footmen, dismissing honest Molly, who waits on common days, and bedizening your table (ordinarily ornamented with willow-pattern crockery) with twopenny-halfpenny Birmingham plate – suppose you pretend to be richer and grander than you ought to be – you are a Dinner-giving Snob.

William Makepeace Thackeray, *The Book of Snobs* (1846).

Mary brought in the fruit on a tray and with it a glass bowl, and a blue dish, very lovely, with a strange sheen on it as though it had been dipped in milk.

'Shall I turn on the light, M'm?'

'No, thank you. I can see quite well.'

There were tangerines and apples stained with strawberry pink. Some yellow pears, smooth as silk, some white grapes covered with a silver bloom and a big cluster of purple ones.

These last she had bought to tone in with the new dining-room carpet.

Katherine Mansfield, 'Bliss' (1918).

One of [his] meals, modelled on an eighteenth-century original, had been a funeral feast to mark the most ludicrous of personal misfortunes. The dining-room draped in black, opened out on to a garden metamorphosed for the occasion, the paths being strewn with charcoal, the ornamental pond edged with black basalt and filled with ink, and the shrub-beries replanted with cypresses and pines. The dinner itself was served on a black cloth adorned with baskets of violets and scabious; candelabra shed an eerie green light over the table and tapers flickered in the chandeliers.

While the hidden orchestra played funeral marches, the guests were waited on by naked negresses wearing only slip-pers and stockings in cloth of silver embroidered with tears.

Dining off black-bordered plates, the company had enjoyed turtle soup, Russian rye bread, ripe olives from Turkey, caviare, mullet botargo, black puddings from Frankfurt, game served in sauces the colour of liquorice and boot-polish, truffle jellies, chocolate creams, plum-puddings, nectarines, pears in grape-juice syrup, mulberries, and black heart-cherries. From dark-tinted glasses they had drunk the wines of Limagne and Roussillon, of Tenedos, Valdepeñas, and Oporto. And after coffee and walnut cordial, they had rounded off the evening with kvass, porter and stout.

J.-K. Huysmans, *Against Nature* (1884).

She then ordered a chicken to be broiled that instant, declaring, if it was not ready in a quarter of an hour, she would not stay for it. Now, though the said chicken was then at roost in the stable, and required the several ceremonies of catching, killing, and picking, before it was brought to the gridiron, my landlady would nevertheless have undertaken to do all within the time; but the guest, being unfortunately admitted behind the scenes, must have been witness to the fourberie; the poor woman was therefore obliged to confess that she had none in the house; 'but, madam,' said she, 'I can get any kind of mutton in an instant from the butcher's.'

'Do you think, then,' answered the waiting-gentlewoman, 'that I have the stomach of a horse, to eat mutton at this time of night? Sure you people that keep inns imagine your betters are like yourselves. Indeed, I expected to get nothing at this wretched place. I wonder my lady would stop at it. I suppose none but tradesmen and grasiers ever call here.' The landlady fired at this indignity offered to her house; however, she suppressed her temper, and contented herself with saying, 'Very good quality frequented it, she thanked heaven!' 'Don't tell me,' cries the other, 'of quality! I believe I know more of people of quality than such as you. – But, prithee, without troubling me with any of your impertinence, do tell me what I can have for supper; for, though I cannot eat horse-flesh, I am really hungry.' 'Why, truly, madam,' answered the landlady, 'you could not take me again at such a disadvantage; for I must confess I have nothing in the house, unless a cold piece of beef, which indeed a gentleman's footman and the post-boy have almost cleared to the bone.' 'Woman,' said Mrs Abigail (so for shortness we will call her), 'I entreat you not to make me sick. If I had fasted a month, I could not eat what had been touched by the fingers of such fellows. Is there nothing neat or decent to be had in this horrid place?' 'What think you of some eggs and bacon, madam?' said the landlady. 'Are your eggs new laid? are you certain they were laid to-day? and let me have the bacon cut very nice and thin; for I can't endure anything that's gross. – Prithee try if you can do a little tolerably for once, and don't think you have a farmer's wife, or some of those creatures, in the house.' – The landlady began then to handle her knife; but the other stopt her, saying, 'Good woman, I must insist upon your first washing your hands; for I am extremely nice, and have been always used from my cradle to have everything in the most elegant manner.'

Henry Fielding, *Tom Jones* (1749).

'I cannot pretend that stealing is right'

Mr Majid looked at him for a few seconds then said, So what can I do you for?

The boy bent down to the side of the counter and picked up a pint of milk from the crate there.

Thirty-three, said Mr Majid.

And have you got any matches?

Wee box?

Aye: do fine. A box of Bluebells was put down beside the milk. How much is that so far?

Forty-three.

The boy took money from his pocket, dumped it on the counter, and slid the coins across to Mr Majid as he counted: Twenty, five, five, ten, one, one, one. He looked at what he was left with. What have you got for seventeen? Mr Majid shrugged, waved his non-smoking hand around the shop. The boy looked at the shelves that went as high as the ceiling, the boxes of fruit and veg ranged along the bottom of them, and the freezer units and sweet display-racks in the middle of the floor. The girl was pottering about the babyfoods. The boy shouted over his shoulder, What do you want for seventeen pence?

I don't know, she replied. Something chocolate.

A Mars bar, Mr Majid?

Twenty.

Two Milky Ways?

Ten each.

A Twix then?

He took a long drag, looking at the boy over the top of his specs. Nineteen, he said.

Not seventeen?

He blew out a jet of smoke. Okay, you can owe me.

Ach, that would be great, said the boy. Ta very much.

The next time you're in . . .

Aye, sure thing, said the boy, picking up the milk, matches and Twix.

The girl opened the shop door and called, Bye for now, as she went out. The boy started to walk after her.

Mr Majid stubbed his fag out under the counter somewhere. Have a nice day, he said, and, as the boy left the shop, went back through the bead curtain.

Outside, the girl was already on the pavement, looking back, waiting for the boy. He crossed over to her slowly, and as he caught up with her she headed for the stairdoor. Once inside, they let it swing behind them, then immediately they ran: along the passageway, up both flights of stairs, through the flatdoor, down the corridor and into their room. She collapsed on the bed, him on the floor, and they were both laughing away, gasping for breath, in between. After half a minute they calmed down.

Well, he said, What did you get?

She sat up on the bed and started pulling things out of the pockets of her coat. Streaky bacon, marge, half a dozen eggs . . .

Eggs! Jesus, how do did you manage them?

I have my methods . . . Now then: tin of tuna, beans . . . hold on, what's this? Processed peas? Shit, I meant to get beans; must've picked up the wrong tin.

Never mind, never mind. Anything else? I mean did you get bread or anything?

She reached inside her coat and from under her arm pulled out a small brown loaf. She held it up to him on the palms of her hands, grinning.

Brilliant, he said, High in fibre. Health-conscious even now.

The little extra for quality goods is always worth it.

Little extra? Jesus, did you see that? Thirty-three for a pint of milk: it's criminal!

Duncan McLean, 'Shoebox' (1992).

I cannot pretend that stealing is right. I can only say that on this occasion it did not look like stealing to the hungry four, but appeared in the light of a fair and reasonable business transaction. They had never happened to learn that a tongue – hardly cut into – a chicken and a half, a loaf of bread, and a syphon of soda-water cannot be bought in shops for half-a-crown. These were the necessary of life which Cyril handed out of the larder window when, quote unobserved and without hindrance or adventure, he had led the others to that happy spot. He felt that to refrain from jam, apple turnovers, cake and mixed candied peel was a really heroic act – and I agree with him. He was also proud of not taking the custard pudding, – and there I think he was wrong, – because if he had taken it there would have been a difficulty about returning the dish; no one, however starving, has a right to steal china pie-dishes with little pink flowers on them. The soda-water syphon was different. They could not do without something to drink, and as the maker's name was on it they felt sure it would be returned to him wherever they might leave it.

E. Nesbit, *Five Children and It* (1957).

I had no time for verification, no time for selection, no time for anything, for I had no time to spare. I stole some bread, some rind of cheese, about half a jar of mincemeat (which I tied up in my pocket-handkerchief with my last night's slice), some brandy from a stone bottle (which I decanted into a glass bottle I had secretly used for making that intoxicating fluid, Spanish-liquorice-water, up in my room: diluting the stone bottle from a jug in the kitchen cupboard), a meat bone with very little on it, and a beautiful round compact pork pie.

Charles Dickens, *Great Expectations* (1816).

She told me once that when she was a very little girl there was going to be a dinner-party at home and she was left alone with some tempting custards, ranged in their glasses upon a stand. She stood looking at them and the thought came into her mind: 'What *would* be the consequence if [I] should eat one of them?' A whimsical sense of the dismay it would cause took hold of her she thought of it again and scarcely knowing what she was about – she put forth her hand, and – took a little from the top of each! She was discovered – the sentence upon her was – to eat all the remaining custards, and to hear the company told the reason why there were none for them! The poor child hated custards for a long time afterwards.

Thomas Carlyle, *Reminiscences* (1881).

EVANS THE DEATH

Laughs high and aloud in his sleep and curls up his toes as he sees, upon waking fifty years ago, snow lie deep on the goosefield behind the sleeping house; and he runs out into the field where his mother is making Welshcakes in the snow, and steals a fistful of snowflakes and currants and climbs back to bed to eat them cold and sweet under the warm, white clothes while his mother dances in the snow kitchen crying out for her lost currants.

Dylan Thomas, *Under Milk Wood* (1954).

In summer the pet pastime of the boys of Dawson's Landing was to steal apples, peaches, and melons from the farmer's fruit wagons – mainly on account of the risk they ran of getting their heads laid open with the butt of the farmer's whip. Tom was a distinguished adept at these thefts-by-proxy. Chambers did his stealing, and got the peach stones, apple cores, and melon rinds for his share.

Mark Twain, *Pudd'nhead Wilson* (1894).

I came across excellent blackberries, – ate of them heartily. It was mid-day, & when I left the brambles, I found I had a sufficient meal so there was no need to go to an inn. Of a sudden it struck me as an extraordinary thing. Here had I satisfied my hunger without payment, without indebtedness to any man. The vividness with which I felt that this was extraordinary seems to me a shrewd comment on a social state which practically denies a man's right to food unless he have money.

George Gissing, *Commonplace Book* (1887).

INDEX OF AUTHORS

FOOD INDEX

anchovies,
  a tasteful breakfast, 60
  delicate rows of, 133
  encountered for first time, 34
apple, 206, 59
  baked, 33
  cool and red, 184
  Cox's Orange Pippin, 83
  dumpling, 30, 82
  obliged to eat, 39
  pie, 86
  sauce, 83
apricots, vulturous eating of, 40
artichokes,
  coeur d', 204
  sea-dust-coloured, 95
asparagus, clo92
  balancing, cg281
  cooked in butter, 91
  dangled, 190
  enormous, 197
  not boiled enough, 143
  old, 101
aubergines,
  strange, 34
  thrown about by baboons, 99

bacon, 33
  cut nice and thin, 208
  not to be wasted, 186
  patron of, 20
  rashers of in stew, 31
  streaky, in pocket, 210
  toasted on a fork, 124
baguette, mistaken for a croissant, 34
baklava, 97
bananas, chocolate-covered frozen, 93
bass, 94
  striped, 91

beans,
  and bacon, 188
  lime, 91
  string, 30
beef, 55
  and ale, land of, 70
  and onion hash, 33
  boil'd, 163
  boiled, contented with, 173
  capable of wrecking happiness, 17
  fillet, 31
  dinner, a shilling, 161
  had to be stringy, 107
  hung, 20
  no better than in Paris, 81
  roast, 33
  sirloins, 56
  steak, give-me-a-thick, 62
  steak, grappled, 194
  stew, may be better things than, 31
beer, 154
beetroot blood, 107
berries, living on, 42
biscuits, 30
  lent by Dowager Countess, 142
  naturally dry, 188
  squashed-fly, 177
bitterns, 143
blackberries, eaten heartily, 213
blancmange, 56,
blini, with caviar, 183
Bloaterre, 49
boar, wild, eleven, 143
boeuf à la gelée, 100
bonito, 63
bouillabaisse, 34
Braten, 201
bratwurst, verging on poison, 97
brawn, presented as a gift, clo92

Food Index

bread, 127
  and butter, glistening, 176
  and butter, in search of, 152
  and butter pudding, 187
  and margarine, wretched, 61
  barleymeal, 85
  black, associated with Popery, 51
  black, soggy, 183
  brown, attempted with awe, 50
  English, 83
  home-made, 31
  hot wheat, 30
  London, deleterious, 102
  none, 181
  not allowed to mistreat, 51
  oatmeal, 85
  request for a gross indecency, 18
  rolls, crammed, 23
  rolls, hot, 30
  Russian rye, 83, 207
  sauce, 83
  Turkish, 105
  twelve pound loaf of, 187
  unleavened, 17
  without butter, 34
Brussels sprouts,
  cluster of, 112
  never turn into wine, 41
boudin blanc, 205
bouillabaisse, 94
bubble-and-squeak, 149
buns,
  ramparts of, 134
  hot buttered, 132
butter,
  (not too much), 51
  plastered, 19
  smelling of clover-blossom, 126
butter-beans, 30
buttermilk, 30

cabbage,
  boiled black, 63
  in water an abomination, 79

juice, 112
  pickled, 105
cake,
  birthday, 68, 69
  Eccles, 86
  handed round on salvers, 65
  hot batter, 30
  hot buckwheat, 30
  like a drug, 70
  Madeleine, 69
  oaten, 145
  plum, 82
  plum, in pocket, 67
  potato, 83
  sweet, 64
  wheaten, 145
calves'feet, best 101
cantaloupes, 30
  feelings for deeper than appetite, 40
Canetons à la mode d'Amblève, 158
capons, one thousand, seven hundred, 143
caramels, 67
caraway seeds, on Jewish bread, 83
carp, 60
carrots,
  cold, thrown quietly out of window, 22
cauliflowers, 95
caviare, 203, 207
  never minded, 195
cayenne pepper, in tortures with, 87
celery,
  Lake's, 92
  like fennel, 95
  sounds like stepping on a basket, 54
  twelve bunches, 90
Chaat, 149
Champagne, 153, 170
  can drink nothing but, 196
  like ginger ale without ginger, 192
chard, potted, 60
cheese,
  Bleu d'Auvergne, 43
  Brin d'amour, 43
  cake, 171, 205

Food Index

Food Index

steak,
  a favourite dish, 33
  eaten by Eulopean, 90
  like the sole of a shoe, 80
  not cooked if brought 'at once', 161
stew, 183
  eaten slowly, gravely, silently, 31
  strong and smelly preferred, 33
  subtraction, 28
stout, 147, 145
strawberry
  acid, 101
  like a large beautified, 29
  too rich to be eaten much of, 39
  tossed by greasy paws, 103
strawberries,
  'British Queen', 153
  currants more refreshing than, 39
  large as a reticule, 65
  seemed discontented, 173
succotash, 30
sugar,
  fragrant, 33
  liberal helping of, 19
  lump or pounded, 73
  melon, 40
  not at all cared for, 25
sugar-peas, 89
sushi, 63
swaddy, a horny pink fellow, 61
sweet and sour pork: a batter musket
  ball, 89
sweet potato, forbidden the company of,
  86
sweetbread, 143

tacos, 93
tangerines, 206
taramasalata,
  challenging, 34
  fountain of youth in, 97
tart,
  Bakewell, 86
  raspberry, 129

walnut, 205
tea,
  a deliverer, 70
  acceptable to strict Hindu, 17
  cheering, 74
  China, none in Bournemouth, 72
  dissipates frowardness, 151
  green, a slow poison, 72
  despiser of, 20
  Indian, 74
  instead of ale and meat, 70
  kindly, 71
  no Latin word for, 74
  Oolong, vital, 71
  originally quite good, 72
  partaken of . . . or not, 132
  ridiculed, 70
  should be back in the mule, 74
  so fond of, 71
  swilled, 23
  favourable to intellectual expression, 78
  thank God for, 71
  weak, 73
thyme, 135
toast, 53, 180
  eloquent smell of, 53
  instead of vegetables, 161
  not enough, 204
  stale, an abomination, 52
  with dripping, 53
tomatoes, 30
  erroneously stuffed, 18
  for chutney, 99
  offensive, 177
tongue, 56, 130
  hardly cut into, 211
  roasted with udder, 58
tournedos, 204
treacle,
  great charm of, 67
  tart, 82
trout,
  fresh, for supper, 63
  unusually recriminatory, 61

REFERENCES AND
COPYRIGHT NOTICES

Exhaustive efforts have been made to secure permissions, but the Editors may not always have succeeded in tracking the relevant copyright holder. We apologise for any omission: notification of such should be address to the Editors c/o the publisher

Adams, D. (1986) *The Hitchhikers Guide to the Galaxy*, London: William Heinemann. Copyright © Douglas Adams, 1986. Reprinted by permission of Pan Macmillan, London.

Alam, M.Y. (2002) *Kilo*, Glasshoughton: Route. Copyright © M.Y. Alam. Printed with permission of the author.

Alcott, L.M. (2004 [1868]) *Little Women*, London: Penguin.

Ali, M. (2003) *Brick Lane*, London: Doubleday. Copyright © 2003 by Monica Ali. Reprinted with the permission of The Random House Group and Scribner, an imprint of Simon & Schuster Adult Publishing.

Allen, W. (1983) *Four Films of Woody Allen*, London: Faber & Faber.

Amis, M. (1981) *Other People: A Mystery Story*, London: Penguin. Copyright © Martin Amis 1984. Reproduced by permission. All rights reserved.

Atwood, M. (1990 [1979]) *The Edible Woman*, London: Virago Press. Copyright © O.W. Toad Ltd. 1969, 1980. Reproduced with permission of Curtis Brown Group Ltd, London.

Atwood, M. (1996) *Alias Grace*, London: Virago Press. Copyright © O.W. Toad Ltd, 1966. Used by permission of Doubleday, a division of Random House and Bloomsbury, London.

Austen, J. (1991 [1815]) *Emma*, London: Everyman's Library.

Auster, P. (1989) *Moon Palace*, London: Faber and Faber. Copyright © Paul Auster, 1989. Used by permission of Viking Penguin, a division of Penguin Group (USA) Inc.

Ayckbourn, A. (1977 [1975]) 'Living Together' in *The Norman Conquest*, London: Chatto & Windus. Reprinted by permission of the Random House Group.

Banville, J. (2005) *The Sea*, London: Picador. Copyright © John Banville (2005) Reprinted with permission of Pan Macmillan.

Barnes, J. (1989) *A History of the World in 10½ Chapters*, London: Jonathan Cape. Reprinted with permission of author.

Barthes, R. (1992 [1957]) *Mythologies*, Paris: Editions du Seuil. Copyright © Jonathan Cape. Reprinted by permission of The Random House Group Ltd.

Bates, H.E. (1972) *An Autobiography: The Ripening World*, London: Methuen. Reproduced by permission of Pollinger Limited and Evensford Productions Ltd.

Beecher, H.W. (1862) *Eyes and Ears*, New York: Tichnor.

Belloc, H. (1926 [1908]) 'On Tea' in *On Nothing and Kindred Subjects*, London: Methuen & Co. Ltd.

Bennett, A. (1976) F. Swinnerton (ed.) *The Journals of Arnold Bennett*, London: Penguin.

Bennett, A. (1990) *Writing Home*, London: Faber & Faber (1994). Copyright © Forelake Ltd 1990.

Benson, E.F. (2004 [1935]) *Mapp and Lucia*, London: Penguin. Copyright © E.F. Benson. Reproduced by permission of A.P. Watt on behalf of The Executors of the Estate of K.S.P. McDowall.

Blackwood, C. (1984) *Corrigan*, New York: New York Review Books. Copyright © 1984, Caroline Blackwood. Reproduced by permission. All rights reserved.

Borrow, G. (1984 [1862]) *Wild Wales*, London: Century.

Boswell, J. (1950 [1763]) *Boswell's London Journal 1762–1763*, London: Heinemann.

Boswell, J. (1985 [1786]) *The Journal of a Tour to the Hebrides*, Harmondsworth: Penguin.

Boswell, J. (1980 [1791]) *Life of Johnson*, Oxford: Oxford University Press.

Bowen, E. (1993 [1923]) *Collected Stories*, London: Vintage. Reproduced with permission of Curtis Brown Group Ltd, London on behalf of the Estate of Elizabeth Bowen.

Bowen, E. (1976 [1935]) *The House in Paris*, Harmondsworth: Penguin. Copyright © Elizabeth Bowen 1935. Reproduced with permission of Curtis Brown Group Ltd, London on behalf of the Estate of Elizabeth Bowen

Boyle, T.C. (1995) *The Tortilla Curtain*, London: Penguin. Copyright © T. Coraghessan Boyle. Used by permission of Viking Penguin, a division of Penguin Group (USA) Inc.

Brand, C. (2005 [1964]) *Nurse Matilda*, London: Bloomsbury. Copyright © Christianna Brand, 1964. Reprinted by permission of A.M. Heath & Co. Ltd.

Brenan, G. (1963 [1957]) *South from Granada*, Harmondsworth: Penguin. Copyright © G. Brenan.

Brillat-Savarin, J.-A., (1994 [1825]) Anne Drayton (trans.) *The Physiology of Taste*, London: Penguin. Copyright © Anne Drayton.

Brontë, A. (1968 [1848]) *The Tennant of Wildfell Hall*, Oxford: Oxford University Press.

Brontë, C. (1907 [1847]) *Jane Eyre*, London: The Shakespeare Head Press.

Brontë, C. (1939 [1849]) *Shirley*, London: John Murray.

Brontë, C. (1907 [1853]) *Villette*, London: T. Nelson & Sons.

Burke, T. (1941) *English Night Life*, London: Batsford.

Burton, R. (2001 [1621]) *Anatomy of Melancholy*, New York: NYRB Classics.

Butler, S. (1968) *The Notebooks of Samuel Butler*, New York: AMS Press.

Calvino, I. (1979) *Mr Palomar*, London: Vintage. Copyright © Harcourt Brace Jovanovich, Inc.

Carey, P. (1988) *Oscar and Lucinda*, London: Faber & Faber. Copyright © Peter Carey. Reprinted by permission of Faber & Faber Ltd.

Carlyle, T. (1997 [1881]) *Reminiscences*, Oxford: Oxford University Press.

Carroll, L. (1954 [1872]) *Through the Looking-Glass*, London: The Heirloom Library.

Cather, W. (2006 [1922]) *One of Ours*, London: Virago. Copyright © The Estate of Willa Cather.

Cather, W. (1991 [1923]) *A Lost Lady*, London: Virago. Copyright © The Estate of Willa Cather.

Cervantes, M. de, (1992 [1604]) *Don Quixote*, Oxford: Oxford University Press.

Chaucer, G. (1960 [c.1380s]) N. Coghill (trans.) *The Canterbury Tales*, Harmondsworth: Penguin.

Cheever, J. (1984 [1946]) 'The Chimera' from *The Stories of John Cheever*, London: Jonathan Cape. Reprinted by permission of The Random House Group Ltd.

Chesterton, G.K. (1934) 'The Poet and the Cheese' from *A Miscellany of Men* in *More Essays by Modern Masters*, London: Methuen.

Chesterton, G.K. (1937) *Autobiography*, London: Hutchinson.

Chesterton, G.K. (1939) 'On Pleasure Seeking' and 'The Appetite of Earth' in *Selected Essays*, London: Collins.

Cisneros, S. (2004 [1984]) *The House on Mango Street*, Copyright © Sandra Cisneros. Published by Vintage Books a division of Random House, Inc., and in hardcover by Alfred A. Knopf in 1994. Reprinted by permission of Susan Bergholz Literary Services, New York. All rights reserved. Reprinted with permission.

Cobbett, W. (1979 [1830]) *Rural Rides*, Harmondsworth: Penguin.

Coleridge, S.T. (1895) E.H. Coleridge (ed.) *Letters of Samuel Taylor Coleridge*, London: William Heinemann.

Collins, W. (1995 [1884]) *I Say No*, Stroud: Sutton Publishing.

Connolly, C. (1999 [1944]) *The Unquiet Grave*, New York: Persea Books. Copyright © Cyril Connolly. Reproduced by permission of the author c/o Rogers, Coleridge and White, 20 Powis Mews, London.

Cook, Capt. J. (1999 [1769]) P. Edwards (ed.) *The Journals*, London: Penguin.

Conroy, F. (1995 [1993]) *Body & Soul*, London: Penguin.

Cowper, W. in Rhys. E. (ed.) *The Letters of William Cowper* (1925), J.M. Dent.

Crace, J. (2002 [2001]) *The Devil's Larder*, London: Viking. Copyright © Jim Crace, 2001. Reprinted by permission of Penguin Books Ltd.

Croft-Cooke, R. (1960) *English Cooking: A New Approach*, Copyright © English Cooking: A New Approach, 1960, London: W.H. Allen.

Dahl, R. (1984) *Boy: Tales of Childhood*, London: Jonathan Cape Ltd and Penguin Books Ltd.

Deighton, L. (2005 [1964]) *Funeral in Berlin*, London: Harper Collins. Copyright © Len Deighton 1964. Reprinted by kind permission of Jonathan Clowes Ltd, London, on behalf of Pluriform Publishing Company BV.

Dickens, C. (1968 [1836]) 'A Christmas Dinner' and 'Public Dinners' in *Sketches by Boz*, London: Everyman's Library.

Dickens, C. (1992 [1838]) *Oliver Twist*, London: Everyman's Library.

Dickens, C. (1994 [1844]) *Martin Chuzzlewit*, London: Everyman's Library.

Dickens, C. (1991 [1850]) *David Copperfield*, London: Everyman's Library.

Dickens, C. (2003 [1853]) *Bleak House*, London: Penguin.

Dickens, C. (1992 [1861]) *Great Expectations*, London Everyman's Library.

Doyle, R. (1998 [1991]) *The Van*, London: Secker and Warburg. Reprinted by permission of The Random House Group Ltd, by Viking Penguin, a division of Penguin Group (USA) Inc. and by John Sutton Management.

Dunmore, H. (2002 [2001]) *The Siege*, London: Penguin. Copyright © by Helen Dunmore. Reprinted by permission of Grove/Atlantic, Inc. and A.P. Watt Literary Agents.

Durrell, L. (2000 [1945]) *Prospero's Cell*, London: Faber & Faber. Copyright © Lawrence Durrell 1945. Reproduced with permission of Curtis Brown Group Ltd, London on behalf of the Estate of Lawrence Durrell.

Earle, A. (1972) 'Nursery Memories' in Morny, C. (ed.) *A Wine and Food Bedside Book*, London: The International Wine and Food Publishing Company. Reprinted with permission.

Ecclesiasticus, Authorised King James Version (1611).

Eliot, C. (1910 [1896]) 'The Happy Life' from *The Durable Satisfactions of Life*, New York: Crowell.

Eliot, G. (1998 [1859]) *Adam Bede*, Oxford: Oxford University Press.

Eliot, G. (1992 [1860]) *The Mill on the Floss*, London: Everyman's Library.

Eliot, G. (1993 [1861]) *Silas Marner*, London: Everyman's Library.

Ellis, B.E. (1991) *American Psycho*, London: Pan Books. Copyright © Bret Easton Ellis.

Ellmann, L. (1988) *Sweet Deserts*, Harmondsworth: Penguin. Copyright © Lucy Ellmann 1988. Reproduced with permission.

Eugenides, J. (2002) *Middlesex*, London: Bloomsbury. Copyright © Jeffrey Eugenides.

Fielding, H. (2005 [1749]) *Tom Jones*, London: Penguin.

Fitzgerald, F.S. (2004 [1922]) *The Beautiful and Damned*, London: Penguin. Reprinted with permission.

Fitzgibbon, T. (1982) *With Love*, London: Century Publishing Co. Ltd. Copyright © Theodora Fitzgibbon. Reprinted with permission.

Flaubert, G. (1982 [1857]) A. Russell (trans.) *Madam Bovary: The Story of a Provincial Life*, Harmondsworth: Penguin. Copyright © Alan Russell (1950). Reprinted by permission of Penguin Books Ltd.

Flaubert, G. (1982 [1877]) R. Baldick (trans.) 'A Simple Heart' in *Three Tales*, Harmondsworth: Penguin. Reprinted by permission of Penguin Books Ltd.

Fleming, I. (2002 [1953]) *Casino Royale*, Copyright © Glidrose Productions Ltd 1953. Reprinted with the permission of Ian Fleming Publications Ltd.

Ford, R. (1927 [1846]) *Gatherings from Spain*, London: J.M. Dent.

Forster, E.M. (1947 [1910]) *Howard's End*, London: Edward Arnold. Printed by permission of The Provost and Scholars of King's College, Cambridge and the Society of Authors as their literary representatives of the Estate of E.M. Forster.

Forster, E.M. (2000 [1924]) *A Passage to India*, London: Penguin. Copyright © The Provost and Scholars of King's College, Cambridge.

France, A. (1881[1908]) (L. Hearn trans.), *The Crime of Sylvestre Bonnard*, New

York: Harper & Bros.

Franzen, J. (2001) *The Corrections*, London: Fourth Estate. Copyright © Jonathan Franzen. Reprinted by permission of The Susan Golomb Literary Agency.

Frazier, C. (1997) *Cold Mountain*, London: Hodder& Stoughton. Copyright © Charles Frazier.

French, M. (1977) *The Women's Room*, London: Summit Books Ltd. Copyright © Marilyn French. Printed by permission of author.

Gaskell, E. (1970 [1848]) *Mary Barton*, Harmondsworth: Penguin.

Gaskell, E. (1993 [1853]) *Cranford*, Ware: Wordsworth Editions Ltd.

Gissing, G. (1905 [1903]) *The Private Papers of Henry Rycroft*, London: Archibald Constable & Co. Ltd.

Gissing, G. (1962) J. Korg (ed.) *George Gissing's Commonplace Book*, New York: New York Public Library.

Goidel, A. (1946) *Alphabet for Odette*, London: Methuen & Co.

Golding, L. (1972) 'There Were No Table Napkins' in Morny. C (ed.) *A Wine and Food Bedside Book*, London: The International Wine and Food Publishing Company. Reprinted with permission.

Grahame, K. (1979 [1908]) *The Wind in the Willows*, London: Methuen Children's Books Ltd.

Graves, R. (1990 [1929]) *Goodbye to all That*, London: Penguin. Copyright © Trustees of the Robert Graves Copyright Trust. Reprinted with permission of Carcanet Press Ltd.

Grayson, D. (1929 [1907]) *Adventures in Contentment*, London: Melrose.

Greene, G. (1974 [1973]) *The Honorary Consul*, Harmondsworth: Penguin. Copyright © Graham Greene. Reproduced by permission of David Higham Associates.

Hamerton, P. G. (1902 [1873]) *The Intellectual Life*, London: Little, Brown.

Hardy, T. (1991 [1874]) *Far from the Madding Crowd*, London: Everyman's Library.

Hardy, T. (1984 [1891]) *Tess of the D'Urbervilles*, London: Everyman's Library.

Hawthorne, N. (1988 [1852]) *The Blithedale Romance*, Oxford: Oxford University Press.

Hawthorne, N. (1998 [1851]) *The House of Seven Gables*, Oxford: Oxford University Press.

Hazlitt, W. (1827) 'On the Want of Money' in *New Oxford Book of English Prose*, Oxford: Oxford University Press.

Henry, O. (1907) 'Cupid à la Carte' in *Heart of the West*, New York: The McClure Company.

Hollinghurst, A. (1988) *The Swimming-Pool Library*, Chatto & Windus. Reprinted by permission of The Random House Group Ltd.

Holmes, O.W. (2004 [1891]) *Over the Teacups,* Whitefish: Kessinger Publishing Co.

Hubbard, K. (1995) *The Best of Kin Hubbard,* Indiana University Press.

Hunt, L. (1876) 'Jack Abbott's Breakfast' and 'The Inside of an Omnibus' in *Men, Women and Books,* London: Smith, Elder & Co.

Hunt, L. (1865 [1841]) *The Seer: Or Common Places Refreshed*, Boston: Roberts.

Hunt, L. (1903) 'Tea-drinking' in *Essays,* London: Walter Scott Ltd.

Huxley, A. (1927 [1924]) 'Uncle Spencer' in *The Little Mexican,* London: Chatto & Windus. Copyright © Renewed 1951 by Aldous Huxley. Reprinted by permission of George Borchardt, Inc., for the Estate of Aldous Huxley.

Huxley, A. (1994 [1921]) *Crome Yellow,* London: Flamingo. Copyright © 1921 by Aldous Huxley. Reprinted by permission of Georges Borchardt, Inc., for the Estate of Aldous Huxley.

Huysmans, J.-K. (1966 [1884]) R. Baldick (trans.) *Against Nature,* Harmondsworth: Penguin.

Irving, W. (1996 [1820–1]) 'The Christmas Dinner' in *The Sketch-Book of Geoffrey Crayon, Gent,* Oxford: Oxford University Press.

Isherwood, C. (1975 [1935]) *Goodbye to Berlin,* London: The Hogarth Press. Copyright © Christopher Isherwood.

James, C. (1980) *Unreliable Memoirs,* London: Picador. Copyright © Clive James 1979. Printed by permission of PDF on behalf of Clive James.

James, H. (1969 [1881]) *The Portrait of a Lady,* London: Everyman's Library.

James, H. (1985 [1884]) A *Little Tour of France,* Harmondsworth: Penguin.

Janowitz, T. (1986) *Slaves of New York,* London: Pan Books. Copyright © Tama Janowitz.

Jerome, J.K. (1964 [1889]) *Three Men in a Boat,* London: Penguin.

Juster, N. (1988 [1962]) *The Phantom Tollbooth,* London: William Collins. Copyright © Norton Juster. Reprinted by permission of Sll/Sterling Lord Literestic, Inc.

Keats, J. (1935 [1895]) *The Letters of John Keats,* Oxford: Oxford University Press.

Keillor, G. (1986 [1985]) *Lake Wobegon Days,* London: Faber & Faber.

Lamb, C. (1923 [1823]) 'A Dissertation upon Roast Pig' in *The Essays of Elia,* London: Everyman's Library.

Lamb, C. in Marrs, E.W. (ed.) (1978) *The Letters of Charles and Mary Lamb,* Ithaca: Cornell University Press.

Lampedusa, G. di (1963 [1958]) *The Leopard,* London: Collins.

Lanchester, J. (1996) *The Debt to Pleasure,* London: Picador. Copyright © John Lanchester 1996. Reprinted with permission of Pan Macmillan.

Landor, W.S. (2006 [1829]) 'Lucellus and Caesar' from *Imaginary Conversations,* Whitefish: Kessinger Publishing Co.

Lawrence D.H. (1930 [1923]) *Sea and Sardinia*, London: Martin Secker.

Leacock, S. (1940 [1910]) *Literary Lapses*, Harmondsworth: Penguin.

Lebowitz, F. (1977) *Social Studies*, New York: Random House.

Lee, L. (1990 [1959]) *Cider with Rosie*, London: The Hogarth Press. Reprinted by permission of The Random House Group Ltd.

Lessing, D. (1995 [1994]) *Under my Skin*, London: Flamingo. Copyright © 1994 Doris Lessing. Reprinted by kind permission of Jonathan Clowes Ltd, London, on behalf of Doris Lessing.

Levy, A. (2004) *Small Island*, London: Review. Reprinted with permission of David Grossman Literary Agency.

Lewis, C.S. (1967 [1955]) *Prince Caspian*, Harmondsworth: Penguin. Copyright © C. S. Lewis Pte. Ltd, 1951. Extract printed by permission.

Lewis, S. (1991 [1920]) *Main Street*, London: Penguin. Copyright © 1920 by Houghton Mifflin Harcourt Publishing Company and renewed 1948 by Sinclair Lewis. Reprinted by permission of Harcourt Mifflin Harcourt Publishing Company.

Leibling, A.J. (1989 [1938]) Back *Where I Came From*, London: Fourth Estate.

Llewellyn, R. (1983 [1939]) *How Green was my Valley*, London: Michael Joseph. Copyright © Richard Llewellyn 1939. Reproduced by permission of Penguin Books Ltd and Curtis Brown Ltd, New York.

Lucas, E.V. (1906) 'Concerning Breakfast' and 'A Word on Toast' from *Fireside and Sunshine*, London: Methuen.

Lynd, R. (1930 [1923]) 'Afternoon Tea' in *The Blue Lion and Other Essays*, London: Methuen & Co. Ltd.

Mansfield, K. (1924) 'Pension Seguin' in *Something Childish*, London: Constable & Co., Ltd.

Mansfield, K. (191[1918]) 'Bliss' in *The Garden Party of other Stories*, London: Everyman's Library.

Mantel, H. (1988) *Eight Months on Ghazzah Street*, Harmondsworth: Penguin. Copyright © Hilary Mantel, 1988. Reprinted by permission of A.M. Heath & Co. Ltd.

Martel, Y. (2006 [2001]) *Life of Pi*, Edinburgh: Canongate.

Maugham, W.S. (1976 [1951]) 'The Luncheon' and 'The Three Fat Women on Antibes' in *The Complete Short Stories* vol. I, London: Vintage. Reproduced with permission of The Estate of W.S. Maugham.

Maugham, W.S. (2000 [1915]) *Of Human Bondage*, London: Vintage. Reproduced with permission of The Estate of W.S. Maugham.

Maugham, W.S. (2000 [1930]) *Cakes and Ale*, London: Vintage. Reproduced with permission of The Estate of W.S. Maugham.

Maupassant, G. de (1946 [1888]) Harold N.P. Sloman (trans.) 'Madam Husson's May King' from *Boule de Suif and Other Stories*, Harmondsworth: Penguin.

Mayhew, H. (1985 [1861]) *London Labour and the London Poor*, London: Penguin.

McCarthy, M. (1963) *The Group*, London: Weidenfeld & Nicolson.

McCarthy, M. (1965 [1957]) *Memories of a Catholic Girlhood*, London: William Heinemann Ltd. Reprinted by permission of the Random House Group.

McEwan, I. (2007) *On Chesil Beach*, London: Jonathan Cape. Reprinted by permission of The Random House Group.

McLean, D. (1992 [1994]) 'Shoebox' in *Bucket of Tongues*, London: Minerva.

Melville, H. (1961 [1851]) *Moby Dick*, London: The New English Library.

Mikes, G. (1946) *How to be an Alien: A Handbook for Beginners and Advances Pupils*, Harmondsworth: Penguin. Copyright © George Mikes, 1946. Reproduced by permission of Penguin Books Ltd.

Miller, H. (1969 [1934]) *Tropic of Cancer*, London: Panther.

Milne, A.A. (1959 [1942]) 'Golden Fruit' in *A Book of English Essays*, Harmondsworth: Penguin. Copyright © The Estate of C.R. Milne reproduced with permission of Curtis Brown Group Ltd.

Milne, A.A. (1934) 'Lunch' in *More Essays by Modern Masters* London: Methuen. Copyright © The Estate of C.R. Milne reproduced with permission of Curtis Brown Group Ltd.

Milne, A.A. (1930 [1920]) 'Going out to Dinner' from *If I May* London: Methuen. Copyright © The Estate of C.R. Milne reproduced with permission of Curtis Brown Group Ltd.

Milne, A.A. (1929) *Winnie the Pooh*, London: Methuen. Illustrated by E.H. Shepard. Copyright © 1926 by E.P. Dutton, renewed 1954 by A.A. Milne. Reproduced by permission of Dutton Children's Books, A Division of Penguin Young Readers Group, A Member of Penguin Group (USA) Inc.

Mo, T. (1992 [1982]) *Sour Sweet*, London, Vintage.

Montgomery, L.M. (1988 [1908]) *Anne of Green Gables*, Harmondsworth: Penguin.

Morton, H.V. (1933 [1923]) *The Heart of London*, London: Methuen. Copyright © Marion Wasdell and Brian de Villiers. Reprinted by permission of Methuen Publishing Ltd.

Morton, H.V. (1983 [1955]) *A Stranger in Spain*, London: Methuen. Copyright © Marion Wasdell and Brian de Villiers. Reprinted by permission of Methuen Publishing Ltd.

Morton, H. V. (1985 [1927]) *In Search of England*, London: Methuen. Copyright © Marion Wasdell and Brian de Villiers. Reprinted by permission of Methuen Publishing Ltd.

Murdoch, I. (1978) *The Sea, The Sea*, London: Chatto & Windus. Copyright © 1978 Iris Murdoch. Reprinted by permission of The Random House Group and Viking Penguin, a division of Penguin Group (USA) Inc.

Narayan, R.K. (1988 [1956]) 'Coffee Worries' in *A Writer's Nightmare*, Harmondsworth: Penguin.

Némirovsky, I. (2007 [1929]) *David Golder*, Chatto & Windus. Reprinted by permission of The Random House Group Ltd.

Nesbit, E. (1993 [1902]) *Five Children and It*, Ware: Wordsworth Editions Ltd.

Newby, E. (1984) *On the Shores of the Mediterranean*, London: Pan Books.

Nicolson, H. (1942) 'Food' in W. E. Williams (ed.) *A Book of English Essays*, Harmondsworth: Penguin. Reprinted by permission of Juliet Nicolson at The Harold Nicolson Estate.

O'Brien, F. (1993) *The Best of Myles*, London: Flamingo. Copyright © Flann O'Brien. Reprinted by permission of A.M. Heath & Co Ltd.

O'Rourke, P. J. (1993 [1987]) *Bachelor Home Companion: A Practical Guide to keeping House Like a Pig*, New York: Atlantic Monthly Press.

Orwell, G. (1989 [1837]) *The Road to Wigan Pier*, Harmondsworth: Penguin. Copyright © George Orwell, 1937 renewed 1986 by the Estate of Sonia B. Orwell, reproduced by permission of Houghton Mifflin Harcourt Publishing Company.

Orwell, G. (1984 [1936]) 'In Defence of English Cooking' from *The Penguin Essays of George Orwell*, Harmondsworth: Penguin. Copyright © George Orwell, 1943. Reproduced by permission of Bill Hamilton as the Literary Executor of the Estate of the Late Sonia Brownell Orwell and Secker & Warburg Ltd.

Ovid (1955 [AD 8]) *Metamorphosis*, London: Penguin.

Partridge, F. (1983 [1973]) *A Pacifist's War*, London: Robin Clark. Copyright © Frances Partridge. Reproduced by permission of the author c/o Rogers, Coleridge and White Ltd, 20 Powis Mews, London.

Peacock, T.L. (1893 [1831]) *Crotchet Castle*, London: J. M. Dent & Co.

Pearson, H. (1948 [1934]) *The Smith of Smiths: Being the Life, Wit and Humour of Sydney Smith*, Harmondsworth: Penguin

Penrose, A.P.D. (ed.) (1927) *The Autobiography and Memoirs of Benjamin Robert Haydon 1786–1846*, New York: Milton Balch & Co.

Pepys, S. (2000[1661]) *The Diary of Samuel Pepys*, London: Harper Collins.

Pitt-Kethley, F. (2000) *My Schooling*, Tamworth: Tamworth Press. Reproduced with permission by author.

Pliny the Elder (1945 [AD 77]) H. Rackham (trans.) *Natural History*, Harvard: Loeb Classical Library.

Potter, B.(1972 [1908]) *The Tale of Jemima Puddleduck*, London: Frederick Warne & Co.

Pougy, L. de (1986) *My Blue Notebooks*, London: Century Publishing.

Powell, D. (1999 [1944]) *My Home is Far Away*, Vermont: Steerforth Press.

Priestley, J.B. (1934) *English Journey*, London: Heinemann Ltd. Copyright © J.B. Priestley. Excerpt is reproduced by permission of PFD (www.pfd.co.uk) on behalf of J.B. Priestley.

Proust, M. (1954 [1913]) C.K. Scott Moncrieff (trans.), *Remembrance of things Past*, London: Penguin.

Quincey, T. de (1987 [1821]) *Confessions of an English Opium Eater*, London: Penguin.

Rabelais, F. (1955 [1534]) *Gargantua and Pantagruel* London: Penguin.

Reitan, E. A. (ed.) (1987 [1736]) 'Gluttony' in *The Universal Spectator, The Best of the Gentleman's Magazine 1731–1754*, New York: The Edwin Mellen Press.

Repplier, A. (1932) *To Think of Tea!*, Boston: Houghton Mifflin.

Roberts, M. (2001) 'The Cookery Lesson' and 'Les Menus Plaisirs' in *Playing Sardines*, London: Virago. Printed with permission.

Roberts, M. (1993) 'Taking it Easy' and 'The Bishop's Lunch' in *During Mother's Absence*, London: Virago. Printed with permission.

Roth, P. (1971 [1969]) *Portnoy's Complaint*, London: Jonathan Cape. Reprinted by permission of The Random House Group Ltd.

Runyon, D. (1965 [1931]) 'A Piece of Cake' from *Guys and Dolls*, Harmondsworth: Penguin.

Russo, R. (1993) *Nobody's Fool*, London: Chatto & Windus. Reprinted by permission of The Random House Group Ltd.

Russo, R. (2002) 'The Mysteries of Linwood Hart' in *The Whore's Child*, London: Chatto & Windus. Reprinted with permission of The Random House Group Ltd.

Saki (Munro, H. H.) (1963) 'The Chaplet' in *The Bodley Head Saki*, London: The Bodley Head.

Saki (Munro, H. H.) (1913 [1911]) 'The Match-maker' in *The Chronicles of Clovis*, London: The Bodley Head.

Scott, W. (1981 [1814]) *Waverley*, London: Penguin.

Scott, W. (2003 [1815]) *Guy Mannering* London: Penguin.

Shelley, P.B. (1813) 'A Vindication of Natural Diet' in *The Selected Poetry and Prose of Shelley*, Ware: Wordsworth Editions Ltd.

Simons, L. (2007 [1817]) *Journal of a Tour and Residence in Great Britain during the years 1810 and 1811*, London.

Smith, D. (1996 [1949]) *I Capture the Castle*, London: Virago. Reproduced by permission of Film Rights Ltd on behalf of the Estate of Dodie Smith.

Smith, S. (1948 [1875]) in H. Pearson, *The Smith of Smiths: Being the Life, Wit and Humour of Sydney Smith*, Harmondsworth: Penguin.

Smith, S. (1881) in Holland, Lady, *A Memoir of The Rev. Sydney Smith*. New York: Harper & Brothers.

Smollett, T. (1981 [1748]) *The Adventures of Roderick Random*, Oxford: Oxford University Press.

Smollett, T. (1967 [1771]) *The Expedition of Humphrey Clinker*, London: Penguin.

Smollett, T. (1983 [1751]) *The Adventures of Peregrine Pickle*, Oxford: Oxford University Press.

Solzhenitsyn, A, (1962) *One Day in the Life of Ivan Denisovich*, London: Victor Gollancz. Reprinted with permission of The Orion Publishing Group.

Stevenson, R.L. (1994 [1883]) *Treasure Island*, London: Penguin.

Swift, J. (1991 [1726]) *Gulliver's Travels*, London: Everyman's Library.

Swift, J. (1996 [1729]) *A Modest Proposal*, New York: Dover.

Swift, J. (2004 [1704]) *A Tale of a Tub*, London: Penguin.

Swift, J. (2007 [1738]) *Polite Conversations*, London: Hesperus Classics.

Thackeray, W.M. (1900 [1846]) *The Book Of Snobs*, London: Thomas Nelson & Sons.

Thackeray, W.M. (1991 [1847]) *Vanity Fair*, London: Everyman's Library.

Thackeray, W.M. (1864 [1850]) *The History of Pendennis*, Oxford: Humphrey Milford.

Thackeray, W.M. (1865[1850]) *A Little Dinner at Timmins*, London: Smith, Elder.

Theroux, P. (1996) *The Pillars of Hercules*, London: Penguin. Copyright © Cape Cod Scriveners Co., 1995. Reproduced by permission of Penguin Books Ltd.

Thicknesse, P. (1777) *A Year's Journey Through France and Spain*, London: W. Brown.

Thomas, D. (2000 [1954]) *Under Milk Wood*, London: Penguin. Reproduced by permission of David Higham Associates.

Thompson, F. (1979 [1939]) *Lark Rise to Candleford*, Oxford University Press. Reproduced by permission of Oxford University Press.

Tolstoy, L. (1918 [1876]) L. & A. Maude (trans.) *Anna Karenina*, Oxford: Oxford University Press.

Tolstoy, L. (1982 [1869]) R. Edmunds (trans.) *War and Peace*, London: Penguin. Copyright © Rosemary Edmunds 1957, 1978. Reproduced by permission of Penguin Books Ltd.

Toole, J. K. (1980) *A Confederacy of Dunces*, London: Penguin. Copyright © Thelma D Toole, 1980. Reprinted by permission of Penguin Books Ltd.

Townsend, S. (2005 [2004]) *Adrian Mole and the Weapons of Mass Destruction*, London: Penguin. Reprinted with permission.

Trevelyan G. (1893 [1876, 2nd edn) *The Life and Letters of Lord Macaulay*, London: Longmans, Green and Co.

Trollope, A. (1995 [1855]) *The Warden*, London: The Folio Society.

Trollope, A. (1986 [1861]) *Framley Parsonage*, Harmondsworth: Penguin.

Twain, M. (1986 [1894]) *Pudd'nhead Wilson*, Harmondsworth: Penguin.

Twain, M. (1924) Albert Bigelow Paine (ed.) *The Autobiography of Mark Twain*, London: Harper Collins.

Twain, M. (2002 [1893]) *The Diary of Adam and Eve*, London: Hesperus Press Ltd.

Tyler, A. (1982) *Dinner at the Homesick Restaurant*, London: Chatto & Windus. Reprinted by permission of The Random House Group.

Updike, J. (1991 [1960]) *Rabbit, Run*, London: Penguin.

Walton, I. (1939 [1653]) *The Compleat Angler*, Harmondsworth: Penguin.

Webster, J. (1976 [1623]) *The Duchess of Malfi*, London: Dent.

Welty, E. (1998 [1975]) 'The Little Store' in *Stories, Essays and Memoir*, New York: The Library of America.

West, P. (1984) 'Voices of England's Past' in A.M. Rosenthal & A. Gelb (eds) *Great tours and Detours*, London: Ebury Press.

Wilde, O. (1994 [1885]) *The Importance of Being Ernest* and 'Dinners and Dishes' *The Complete Works of Oscar Wilde*, London: HarperCollins.

Willans, G. & Searle, R. (1984 [1958]) *The Compleet Molesworth*, London: Pavilion Books.

Winterson J. (1990 [1985]) *Oranges Are Not the Only Fruit*, London: Pandora.

Winton, T. (1991) *Cloudstreet*, London: Picador. Reproduced by permission.

Wodehouse, P. G. (1993 [1923]) *The World of Psmith Omnibus*. Harmondsworth: Penguin. Copyright © P. G. Wodehouse. Reproduced by permission of the Estate of P.G. Wodehouse c/o Rogers, Coleridge and White Ltd, 20 Powis Mews, London W11 1JN.

Wodehouse, P.G. (1961 [1934]) *Right Ho, Jeeves*, Harmondsworth: Penguin. Copyright © P.G. Wodehouse. Reproduced by permission of the Estate of P.G. Wodehouse c/o Rogers, Coleridge and White Ltd, 20 Powis Mews, London W11 1JN.

Wolfe, T. (1970) *Radical Chic & Mau-Mauing the Flak Catchers*, New York: Bantam Books.

Woodforde, J. (1979 [1802]) *The Diary of a Country Parson 1758–1802*, Oxford: Oxford University Press.

Woolf, V. (1973 [1928]) *A Room of One's Own*, Harmondsworth: Penguin. Reprinted with permission by Society of Authors as the Literary Representative of the Estate of Virginia Woolf.

Woolf, V. (1992 [1927]) *To the Lighthouse*, Harmondsworth: Penguin. Reprinted with permission by Society of Authors as the Literary Representative of the Estate of Virginia Woolf. Copyright © 1927 by Houghton Mifflin Harcourt Publishing Co. and renewed 1954 by Leonard Woolf. Reprinted with permission of the Publisher

Yuan Mei 'The Art of Dining' in F.H. Pritchard (1929) *Great Essays of All Nations*, London: George G. Harrap.

Young, A. (1950 [1789]) 'French Manners and Customs' in *Travels in France*, Cambridge University Press.

Zola, E. (1970 [1876]) L.W. Tancock (trans.) *L'Assommoir*, Harmondsworth: Penguin. Copyright © L.W. Tancock 1970. Reproduced by permission of Penguin Books Ltd.